The Kensington Rune Stone

The Kensington Rune Stone

Its Place in History

by

Thomas E. Reiersgord

ISBN 1-880654-23-7 (hardcover)
ISBN 1-880654-24-5 (trade paperback)

Library of Congress Control No. 2001 130290

Book design by Wendy Holdman
Typesetting by Stanton Publication Services, Inc.
Maps by Matt Kania
Cover design by Mighty Media

To my parents, Bertha and Erwin Reiersgord,

to my wife Camilla, and

to our four children,

Diane, Susan, Robert and Julia

Table of Contents

Part III — The Ojibway

Part IV — The Historical Consequence

preface

THE AUTHENTICITY OF THE INSCRIPTION OF THE
Kensington Rune Stone (or KRS, as I will refer to it) has
been debated ever since the stone was unearthed in 1898.
It was seen by its advocates as proof of Scandinavian exploration
in North America before Columbus, and by its critics as a hoax.
The debate has focused on the runic usages and the language of
the inscription, and not on its content. Its message that told of
finding ten men dead, red with blood, was assumed by both sides
to be the report of an Indian attack.

About a decade ago an alternative interpretation of that message came to my mind, one changing the message from an Indian attack to a report of illness, the Black Death. I began by
studying medieval Scandinavia during the time of the Black
Death. I also learned that modern man generally fails to understand how much the medieval world differed from the modern
era. Critics of the KRS also seem to have assumed that an exploration that could produce the inscription was impossible. To the
contrary, my study supplies many plausible reasons explaining
why and how such an exploration journey could have happened
during that time period.

I developed the hypothesis that the explorers were led west
by Indian guides who followed the same travel routes that later
generations of guides used to show the first post-Columbian explorers the way west. This new interpretation assumed peaceful

contact with the Indians. Because everyone previously assumed that there had been an Indian massacre, no one had looked to Indian history for evidence showing peaceful contact. To my surprise I found much evidence of European contact in Dakota Indian history, reflected in names and traditions originating in the mid-14th century. Also, archaeological evidence has been found showing major changes in the Dakota Indian life style that suggests European influence at that time, centered in the area where I believe that contact occurred. I believe that the broad extent of Dakota material, that in many cases is very specific, supplies persuasive confirmation supporting my new interpretation of the KRS inscription, and the story of its creation.

My presentation in general raises the questions: what is proof, and are cultures evolved spontaneously or do they reflect outside influence? Here, the emergence of new traditions, ceremonial practices, beliefs relating to stones, new methods of agriculture and living styles, all in the mid-14th century, require explanation for their causes. The Dakota record itself attributes these changes to a visitation. Why not accept their accounts as true?

The Ojibway Indians, and possibly other eastern Indian histories, are also involved, not directly with the KRS, but with the activities of Europeans, possibly before, or as part of the KRS exploration, or shortly thereafter. Here again the Indian record, while containing vast amounts of European material, has become more and more evaluated as myth, or of post–Columbian origin, while the early writers who were close enough to the native scene, knew that was not the case.

While obviously you cannot prove the authenticity of the KRS inscription simply because it exists, carved in stone, I believe that at some point the body of other evidence reaches a level that is persuasive enough so that the inscription itself evolves into Exhibit A, to supply the final truth of the story explaining its creation. While many details of the KRS story, and its impact on the future, may be revised after further research, I believe that this book provides a complete enough picture to make the case that the KRS inscription is genuine and that its story is an important part of American history.

Thomas E. Reiersgord
St. Louis Park, Minnesota
March 2, 2001.

⊹ Part 1 ⊹

A New Perspective

Introduction

MY INTEREST IN THE KENSINGTON RUNE STONE (KRS) began many years ago, however, because most historians had labeled it a hoax, it seemed naïve to think otherwise. Perhaps the KRS lingered in my mind because, unlike myths or legends which can change or fade away, the Kensington inscription remained, carved in hard stone. While an inscription doesn't change, our understanding of its meaning and authenticity can. In 1991, an alternative interpretation of the Kensington Rune Stone inscription came to me. Perhaps the inscription was never intended to be a report of a massacre, but instead was simply a description of the death scene of ten men who had died suddenly from a quick acting form of the bubonic plague, the Black Death of the 14th century. I reviewed the inscription and found nothing that was contrary to this new interpretation. After I learned that the pneumonic form of the bubonic plague brought quick death with major hemorrhaging from the lungs and that outbreaks of the Black Death were a common event during the time of the inscription, I was prompted to begin a wider study of history to test this new interpretation, and to perhaps solve the mystery of the Kensington Rune Stone.

I believe that the results of my study will establish that this new interpretation of the Kensington inscription is correct, that it was carved in the 14th century and therefore stands as proof that Europeans had traveled deep into the heart of North America in that period. My study also explains that the Christian nature of Indian legends was the legacy of the explorers' efforts to teach Christianity to the Indians. In addition to that early contact, the inscription's revelation that the bubonic plague was introduced into North America in the 14th century explains why the Indian population of North America suffered a major decline at that time, from which it had made only a modest recovery by the time European settlement began in the 17th century. That severe reduction in the Indian population also destroyed many of the more advanced aspects of Indian civilization that had developed during the period from approximately 1000 to 1400 A.D. The Indians' loss of their more sophisticated social and civil structure, as well as great loss of population, allowed subsistence farmers from Europe the opportunity to gain a foothold in North America without opposition; thus achieving a critical first step that enabled European expansion into North America. For these reasons, the Kensington Rune Stone (KRS) stands as a major document of North American history.

The KRS was found in 1898 near the village of Kensington in Douglas county, Minnesota. A farmer, Olof Ohman, found it while removing an aspen tree that was growing on his farm. When the tree was uprooted, he reported that the stone was discovered lodged within its roots. Ohman's farm is now a park, and a monument stands where the KRS was unearthed. The KRS is the prime focus of the Runestone Museum, established in 1951 in nearby Alexandria, Minnesota.

After the KRS was discovered, it traveled. It was shipped to the Twin Cities, to Chicago, to Washington, D.C., and even to Europe (accompanied by Hjalmar Holand) in order that scholars could study it. Their reports and many other articles and books form what has become a voluminous trove of Kensington Rune Stone materials. Its importance to Minnesotans is emphasized by the fact that from 1910 to as recently as the fall of 2000 articles have appeared in the publications of the Minnesota Historical Society.

Kensington Rune Stone.
This graywacke boulder, carved with runes, was found in 1898 on Olof
Ohman's farm near Kensington, Minnesota. It is housed in its own museum
in Alexandria, Minnesota.
Photograph courtesy of Minnesota Historical Society, 1950.

Two academic historians have written books on the KRS that claim it is a forgery. The first was *The Kensington Stone, A Mystery Solved*, by Erick Wahlgren, a professor of Scandinavian languages at UCLA, in 1958. The second, a decade later, was *The Kensington Rune Stone. New Light on an old Riddle*, by Theodore C. Blegen. Blegen, a professor of history and Dean of the Graduate School at the University of Minnesota, specialized in Norwegian studies. His negative judgment on the inscription's authenticity was very convincing to many people. Most historians have accepted the opinions of these two authors and consider the issue to be closed. As the reader will note, I disagree.

The inscription's English translation has not been in serious dispute. Hjalmar Holand, a scholar who wrote several books advocating the inscription's authenticity, used this translation in his book, *The Kensington Stone: A Study in Pre-Columbian American History* (1932):

The nine lines on the face of the stone read:

1. [We are] 8 Goths [Swedes] and 22 Norwegians on
2. [an] exploration-journey from
3. Vinland over the West [i.e., through the western regions] We
4. had camp by 2 skerries [i.e. by a lake wherein are two skerries] one
5. day's-journey north from this stone
6. We were [out] and fished one day After
7. We came home [we] found 10 [of our] men red
8. with blood and dead Ave Maria
9. Save [us] from evil.

The three lines on the edge of the stone read:

10. [We] have 10 of our party by the sea to look
11. after our ships [or ship] 14 day's-journey
12. from this island Year 1362 (Holand 1932: 6).

Blegen and Wahlgren used the following translation:

1. 8 Swedes and 22 Norwegians on
2. an exploration journey from
3. Vinland westward. We
4. had our camp by 2 rocky islets one
5. day's journey north of this stone.
6. We were out fishing one day.
7. When we came home we found 10 men red
8. with blood and dead. AVM
9. save us from evil.
10. We have 10 men by the sea to look
11. after our ships, 14 days' journey
12. from this island. Year 1362. (Blegen 1968: 11, Wahlgren 1958: 3).

There is, however, one word used in both versions which I believe is an error. It is the word "evil," in line 9, which has been translated to read "save us from evil." I argue that line 9 should be translated as, "save us from illness." The translators adopted the word "evil" from the familiar line of the Lord's Prayer, "deliver us from evil." A better translation of the word found in the inscription is, "ill" or "illness." Translators have assumed that the line was intended to echo the line from the Lord's Prayer, and seem to have reasoned that illness in the medieval period was seen as an evil, and have concluded that the Scandinavian word "illu" or "illy" had both meanings.

My new interpretation of the KRS inscription is based on accepting what it says without making assumptions. Most writers assumed, for over a century, that the KRS inscription told of an attack by Indians. However, there is not one word in the lengthy inscription that mentions Indians, fighting, or killing. Some skeptics have justly argued that if an attack had occurred, then the survivors would have fled for their lives and certainly would not have taken the time to compose and carefully carve an inscription in stone. It is clear from chisel marks on the stone that it was carved from a larger boulder into the shape of a tombstone, creating a flat front and one flat side, while the other side and rear of the boulder were left in the original rough state. Shaping the boulder and carving the inscription, required time, skill and care. A careful reading of the inscription reveals that the interpretation of a "massacre" is merely an inference. Medieval men were very well acquainted with violence and had many words available to describe it, but none are to be found in the KRS inscription. When drafting an inscription that is to be carved in stone it is inappropriate to rely on implication—a direct statement is required.

The KRS inscription describes the appearance of ten men of their party who were found dead, just as the leaders saw the scene when they returned to their camp. By 1362 the Black Death had been ravaging Europe for about 15 years. It was a disease that must have been all too familiar to the explorers, and one which they had good reason to fear. Yet in the fourteenth century neither the cause nor nature of the illness were understood, nor was there even a name for the disease. The term, Black Death, was not used when the disease first appeared. According to Philip Ziegler the earliest known uses of that name were in Sweden in 1555 and only after 1665 in England (Ziegler 1971: 17). In cases of pulmonary bubonic plague, where the victims died quickly and coughed up blood at death, calling the illness the "red death" would have been more appropriate. Because the carver of the KRS had no name for the illness, he could only report the facts. It was the frightful aspect of bleeding in the final stage that prompted him to write that the 10 dead men were "red with blood." It was as precise a report of the cause of death as the author of the inscription could make.

The cause of the plague was a complete mystery to Europeans of the 14th century, so most, in that Church–dominated society, believed it was God's punishment. It is known that some people realized that the plague was contagious and therefore they sought refuge in remote areas to escape the danger. However, people often carried infected fleas with them, and so ended up being stricken after they had fled to what they had hoped would be a place of refuge. The basic bubonic plague was spread by fleas, however, the disease often evolved into the pulmonary form, which was easily spread directly from person to person by droplet transmission, skipping the basic bubonic plague form and the role of the flea.

The pulmonary form nearly always resulted in quick death and discharge of blood. While the ten victims most likely died of the bubonic plague in its pneumonic form, they may have had yet a third form, the septicemic, which always resulted in quick death and also caused its victims to cough up blood from severe hemorrhaging in their lungs. Some medical historians now think that the Black Death of the 14th century in Europe was a combination of the bubonic plague and some other virulent disease, such as anthrax, which also is a disease where death is accompanied with discharge of blood (Twigg 1984: 221).

My new interpretation of the Kensington inscription implies that when the ten men died, the explorers had been camped in a peaceful setting from where it would be convenient to do some fishing. No doubt sustaining a party of 30 men required a substantial quantity of food. When the ten men died, the leaders of the party, probably Christian monks, were confronted with the issue of proper care of the dead. When that issue was resolved, then presumably the survivors left the fishing camp site and returned to their main encampment, which according to the inscription, was located one day's journey south of the place where the men had died. Back at their main camp, they no doubt continued to reflect on what had occurred.

An understanding of the plague and the time of the inscription is necessary as an inscription must be read from its authors' perspective. By 1362, when the inscription was carved, millions of Northern Europeans had died from the plague since it had first reached that region in 1348. The plague continued to flare up for over 150 years after it had begun. Considering the magnitude of that pandemic, anyone from Northern Europe in 1362 would have lived in close proximity to the plague for about 14 years. No other subject could have been more on the mind of the people of that time, yet it remained a mystery. The explorers had no maps and there were no place names known to identify their location. When the ten men died, the explorers had already traveled a long way west, and we can surmise that out of fear and fatigue they then gave up any idea of traveling further on their exploration. Thus, it was the time to make some record to mark how far they had traveled west from Vinland, and to record the reason why their western exploration was at an end. They were in what they saw as a remote wilderness. Small wonder that they also included a prayer seeking protection for themselves from the illness.

The graywacke boulder which became the KRS was probably found on the island where they had their main camp. After the inscription was carved, the stone was likely left standing in that encampment. My investigation leads me to believe that the inscription was carved on an island in Knife Lake, a place whose name reflects Isanti Dakota Indian words that refer to "cutting" and "stone." I believe that the Lake's name is a reference to the KRS, which the Dakota would have considered a cut stone. Knife Lake is located in Kanabec county, southeast of Lake Mille Lacs. According to Isanti Dakota Indian tradition, Knife Lake (Isantamde) was a one day's walk from Lake Mille Lacs or Spirit Lake (Neill 1882: 52). The geographic location described in the inscription matches this information.

The two skerries used as reference points or landmarks in the inscription are the two boulder islands in Lake Mille Lacs—and can be seen from its southerly shore. A skerry is a rocky islet, just as translated in the version of the inscription used by Wahlgren and Blegen. When the author used the words (two skerries) to describe the boulder islands, he again was being as precise as possible considering that he was a stranger in a land where there were many landmarks, none of which had names that he knew. His choice of terms is another example of his care in drafting the inscription. He would have assumed that when looking for a site where two rocky islets could be seen, one day's journey north from the island where the stone was standing, that anyone would understand that he was referring to the two boulder islands in Lake Mille Lacs.

The reason why everyone has heretofore read the KRS inscription as the report of an Indian attack was because when the stone was found in 1898, European settlers in North America had been in hostile conflict with the American Indian population for several centuries. This precedent contributed greatly to the shaping of peoples' attitudes, and their resulting interpretation of the KRS inscription. The erroneous assumption that produced the massacre interpretation simply reflected the attitudes and fears of European-Americans of that period. Rather than reading the inscription from the perspective of the time that it was carved, it was read from the perspective of the time when it was found.

The elaborate theory created by Hjalmar R. Holand in his attempt to explain how the Kensington inscription came to be carved, has also confused the issue. He claimed that an expedition, sent by the King of Norway, sailed into Hudson's Bay and traveled via river to Lake Winnipeg where they sailed south. From there they continued south on the Red River of the North into what is now Minnesota. Holand then postulated that the group headed east on a small stream, and while at a campsite, ten of the group were killed by Indians. Holand assumed that the KRS was carved where it was found which, according to the inscription, would mean that the stone's discovery site was located one day's journey south of the supposed massacre site. Holand's improbable thesis was vulnerable to attack, thus much of the negative writing on the KRS is devoted to ridicule of Holand's thesis. While I believe Holand's thesis to account for the making of the inscription to be wrong, his efforts have preserved the KRS for history, and his linguistic study of the inscription was an important contribution.

Blegen's 1968 book on the Rune Stone contained many useful details about the KRS, including one point supporting my new interpretation. Specifically, Blegen noted in an appendix (quoting from the field notes of Newton Winchell) that a line from the inscription, "AVM, save us from the evil," was a line commonly used in Scandinavia at the burials of Black Death victims (Blegen 1968:150). Because Blegen and everyone else only saw the inscription as a report of an Indian massacre, he failed to literally accept the very clue he included in his book that suggests the truth about the inscription. It is interesting to note that Wahlgren's book, published a decade earlier, did not seem to persuade Blegen that the KRS inscription was a fake. Five years after Wahlgren's book Blegen published a history of the State of Minnesota. He referred to the KRS, describing it by adopting Winston Churchill's famous line: "It is a riddle wrapped in a mystery inside an enigma" (Blegen 1963: 29). By 1968, Blegen had come to a negative judgment, but even then he states that he was not absolutely sure, leaving the issue open with these words: ". . . it is possible that fresh analyses of old sources, made by newer scholarship with the aid of new evidence or altered perspectives, or both, may help to clarify questions that have defeated scholars in the past" (Blegen 1968: 90). I believe that it was my good fortune to have the "altered perspective" that Blegen seemed to anticipate.

In recent years, a few scholars, most notably Robert A. Hall and Richard Nielsen, have written in support of the inscription's authenticity. They have investigated the linguistic criticism of the inscription and have found evidence of 14th century usages of most of the words in the inscription that earlier critics claimed were unknown at that time. In effect, their findings turned the linguistic criticism of the inscription around, because if the inscription was a fake, it meant that the forger had a far greater knowledge of 14th century runic usages than did the critics. While their conclusions appear to be sound, Hall and Nielsen's linguistic studies of the inscription have been rejected or ignored by most historians. One explanation for this dismissal or lack of attention is that few people are acquainted with runic linguistics, and therefore have no basis upon which to judge such a debate. Another reason why their work has been ignored may be because the linguistic issue is not conclusive by itself. To resolve the issue of the KRS, it is necessary that we understand the meaning of the inscription and the context of its origin, and identify the locations referred to in the inscription.

Beyond understanding that the inscription did not tell of an attack, the second new perspective that was essential to solve the KRS mystery was to understand why the geographical references in the inscription have no relationship to the geography of the farm where Olof Ohman discovered the stone. Logically, the inscription must not have been carved at the site where it was found. That realization should have been clear from the beginning, because no one has ever found the waste material that would have been produced when the boulder was initially carved into the shape of the KRS. My review of Dakota Indian history leads me to believe that the Indians carried it with them from its original site when they moved away from the Knife Lake area. Many years later they transported the KRS to the site where it was found, where they gave it a ceremonial burial, and placed an aspen tree, their traditional sacred tree, over the buried stone. The aspen took root, lived, and grew so that its roots reached around the stone. Eventually, it was the removal of that aspen by Olof Ohman which led to the stone's discovery.

Aside from the absence of debris, another reason why it should be clear that the KRS was intentionally buried at the place where it was found is because it was found underground. In Minnesota, in the Kensington area, frost in winter often extends several feet or more deep into the ground, and the movement caused by the frost, followed by thawing in the spring, tends to force buried rocks upward. This is a common problem for Minnesota farmers who have rocky land, as they often encounter newly emerging boulders in their fields in the spring. Because of that phenomenon, a large stone like the KRS, if left on the surface, would not become buried over time, but would remain on or at the surface. Because the KRS was found underground, it follows that someone intentionally buried it there. Skeptics can claim that the forger buried the stone. However, nearly everyone acquainted with Olof Ohman believed him to be sincere and truthful (Blegen 1968: 58, 72, 135, 163). O. J. Breda, a University of Minnesota professor, studied the KRS soon after it was found and made visits to the discovery area. While he concluded that the inscription was a fake, his belief was that the stone had been carved by someone traveling in that area in the 1860's. Breda became acquainted with Olof Ohman, and wrote in a 1910 letter to Warren Upham: "I have never seen any reason to connect Mr. Ohman or any one else now living in the neighbourhood of Kensington, with the forgery in any way. The man who cut the inscription into the stone and buried it in the ground has probably not lived to enjoy the turmoil caused by the discovery of it" (Blegen 1968: 169).

I find it difficult to believe that anyone would create a lengthy inscription in stone as a hoax and then bury it with only a very remote possibility that it would ever be found. It should also be clear that no medieval stone carver would have buried the stone after carving the inscription, as that would defeat his purpose. To answer the question of who buried the KRS, we must look to the local population. In the 14th century, the Dakota Indians occupied the area that became Minnesota, and they continued to live in their native way of life in western Minnesota until the 1860's. In subsequent chapters, we will see that it is most likely that a small group of Dakota Indians buried the KRS near Kensington, probably intending to put its influence behind them, although the Dakota traditions that were related to it remain a major part of Dakota Indian culture.

Vinland—Where the
Journey Began

L
INES 2 AND 3 OF THE KRS INSCRIPTION STATE THAT
its authors were on an exploration journey from "Vinland
Westward." Vinland was the only place name used in the
inscription. The explorers' concept that Vinland (rather than Europe) was their departure point is important. It implies that exploring land west of Vinland was a new idea, and not one in their
minds when they left Europe. Only after being in Vinland for a
significant period of time did they realize that extensive lands lay
to the west. The break in travel from Europe to Vinland, and only
later from Vinland to the west, suggests that the party of explorers who went west was organized by men from several groups
who may have arrived in Vinland at different times, perhaps years
apart.

Two issues about Vinland are particularly relevant to the KRS:
its location, and whether it was known in Scandinavia, especially
within the Church. My conclusion is that Vinland was known in
Scandinavia and in the Church in the 14th century, and that the
name Vinland had become a regional term for the St. Lawrence
Gulf Region at that time. This is significant because the St.
Lawrence Gulf and River offered the only practical route that
Europeans could have used to travel west into the Great Lakes
waterways of North America in the 14th century. It was an easy
route, the same one used by early French explorers to enter into
the heartland of North America centuries later, long before

routes west from the original thirteen colonies were established through the Appalachian Mountains.

Historians have claimed many different places to be the site of Leif Erickson's Vinland. Some remained skeptical about Vinland having ever existed until Helge Ingstad discovered the L'Anse aux Meadows site on the northwestern tip of Newfoundland in 1960. The Ingstad discovery was established archeologically as a site occupied by Scandinavians in about the year 1000. Ingstad concluded: "a number of circumstances indicate that it was at L'Anse aux Meadows that Leif Erickson built his 'large houses' and that northern Newfoundland is the Vinland of the Saga" (Ingstad 1969: 221). Samuel Eliot Morison in *The European Discovery of America. The Northern Voyages*, agreed (Morison 1971: 38). C. W. Ceram, in *The First American*, also agreed, although Ceram withheld judgment on the KRS because, in his view, the evidence used by the skeptics was circumstantial and failed to account for the motivation for forgery (Ceram 1971: 19).

While the L'Anse aux Meadows site confirms the Norse sagas, it is not necessarily proof that the site was Leif Erickson's Vinland. The site is too cold for wild grapes, which inspired the name "Vinland." L'Anse aux Meadows was a logical place for a camp to support exploration and trade into the Gulf of St. Lawrence because it was located at its Atlantic entrance. If parties split up or became separated it would have been a good meeting place. Another logical reason for a camp or support site to be at that location was that it offered a last opportunity for outbound ships to obtain fresh water, hunt game, and prepare for sea travel. L'Anse aux Meadows was probably only a support site established by later visitors because more hospitable land could be reached by following either the Newfoundland or Labrador shorelines to the southwest. That is where we should look for Erickson's Vinland and for the other sites that were occupied for several years by later colonization efforts. The sagas were handed down by oral tradition in an illiterate society. The explorers saw their discoveries as their proprietary property, but they had no way to protect their property interests in their discoveries other than to keep key information secret. Leif Erickson and other Norse explorers who sailed to Vinland had no reason to tell the world the true way to Vinland. Some of the sailing directions may well have been intentionally misleading, with the true interpretation entrusted to a select few. That may explain why most subsequent travelers from Greenland were able to find Vinland in the 11th century, while 20th century writers have been so confused that they have judged its location to be anywhere from Hudson's Bay to Virginia. Similarly, the account in one of the sagas telling of an attack by "unipeds" was probably intended to frighten others from trying to encroach on the newly discovered lands. It may also be that when the sagas note the wind direction they meant in fact the sailing direction.

Therefore, to locate the Norse settlements, it seems best to consider the descriptions of the natural features of the sites together with what is known of the region's geography today, and to examine the records of early post-Columbian explorers in the Gulf region. A reasonable interpretation of Leif Erickson's first voyage might be that after sighting land, he sailed southerly along the Atlantic coast of Labrador until he reached the Strait of Belle Isle, where he entered into the Gulf of St. Lawrence. At that point he had passed two lands, Helluland on his right, and Markland (Newfoundland) on his left. As he entered into the gulf he had two choices: follow the Newfoundland shore or the Labrador shore. Since the Newfoundland shore was more wooded and turned more southerly, that was his choice. After reaching the western end of Newfoundland, he probably correctly judged that it was an island. Instead of rounding Newfoundland, he decided instead to change his plan and head north to follow the Labrador shore. This plan would keep him within what he likely had noted were the quieter gulf waters. At this point the Leif Erickson Greenland saga says: "They sailed away out to sea from this landfall in a northeast wind. And when they were out to sea two days they came in sight of land again. They held in to this land (presumably following a coastline) and came to an island that lay north of the land" (Reman 1990: 24). That land was Leif Erickson's Vinland. Some have assumed that because of the northeast wind that Erickson must have headed south. However, if you regard the direction northeast in the saga as the sailing direction, and interpret the language saying that the island they encountered lay north of the land to mean where they had made their prior landfall and from where they had departed two days earlier, headed northerly, then you have a route that goes from the southwestern end of Newfoundland, northeast to the Labrador Coast, and then southwesterly following along that coast until you come to Anticosti Island. That route within the gulf was the same one that Jacques Cartier sailed on his first recorded voyage in 1534, and for which he is remembered as the discoverer of Anticosti Island. Probably the same factors that prompted Leif Erickson also prompted Cartier. Anticosti Island was easy to find. Anyone entering the gulf through the Strait of Belle Isle and following the Labrador shore would find it. Finding the way back was equally easy. A simple route was a basic necessity when one was traveling in an area of usually heavy fog, with illiterate sailors and few navigational instruments.

Another good reason to identify Anticosti Island as Vinland is because we can presume that it had a climate warm enough for grapevines, and Erickson named his island Vinland because grapevines were found there. Anticosti is warmer due to ocean currents. The U.S. Navy publication, *St. Lawrence Pilot for 1917,* provides many details about the gulf area, including this observation about the climate of Anticosti: "The climate of Anticosti is far less severe than that of the mainland or even of Quebec; the winter is more temperate, and the summer is cooler" (USN 1917: 239). Cartier reported finding grapevines in the Quebec area in 1535, so if Anticosti's climate is less severe than Quebec's, wild grapevines could have grown there as well. In 1748, Peter Kalm, a Scandinavian botanist and explorer, noted that "wild grapevines grow quite plentifully in the wood," on Isle of Orleans, opposite Quebec (Kalm 1937: 481).

The eastern end of Anticosti Island has several physical features that match the description of the island that Leif Erickson called Vinland. The landmarks of Vinland mentioned in the sagas include a cape with extensive areas of sand and a lake with a river flowing from it into the sea. The river enabled the sailors to tow their ship into the lake, where it was secured (Reman 1990: 24). The name of the eastern tip of Anticosti Island is East Cape. The *St. Lawrence Pilot* describes it thus: "A conspicuous patch of sand on the face of a steep slope . . . and the cliff westward of the patch rises to a height of 90 feet, falling again to 45 feet in a projection that forms the northern side of Wreck Bay." The description of Wreck Bay continues: "There is a lake of fresh water close inshore of the landing place" (USN 1917: 240–1). A body of fresh water next to ocean waters would usually have an outlet flowing from the lake to the salt water, as otherwise the lake water would not be fresh. I would judge that the lake described in the *St. Lawrence Pilot* at the east end of Anticosti is the same lake mentioned in the Erickson saga.

The Greenland and Icelandic sagas also tell of other voyages made to Vinland in the years after Leif Erickson. These expeditions were serious attempts at colonization. Whole families migrated. Cattle were brought because most of the Icelandic and Greenland food supply came from livestock and fish. While L'Anse aux Meadows did yield artifacts which were dated to the saga period, it is significant to note that no evidence of cattle was found at that site.

Several years after Leif Erickson's voyage, a man named Thorfinn Karlsefini sponsored a large colonizing expedition to Vinland that sailed further south and west, presumably beyond Anticosti. Part of his group of colonists founded a settlement which they named "Straumfjord" (Streamfjord), a name chosen because it described the strong current at the mouth of the fjord where their settlement was located. Fjords are rare in the St. Lawrence region, and probably the only waterway in the area that fits that description is the lower Saguenay River which flows from the north into the St. Lawrence Gulf, about 250 miles southwest of Anticosti Island. Probably the settlement Karlsefini named Straumfjord was at the mouth of the Saguenay River, which today is the community of Tadoussac.

The *St. Lawrence Pilot* for 1917 confirms that the Saguenay River does resemble a fjord and that strong currents are a serious danger at the river's mouth as it enters the St. Lawrence. The Navy description was:

> Saguenay River . . . is a very remarkable and extraordinary river, inasmuch as it nearly resembles a long and narrow mountain loch for the first 50 miles above its confluence with the St. Lawrence.

> In this distance the Saguenay is from 1,200 yards to 2 miles wide, filling up a deep transverse valley through mountains of sienitic granite and gneiss. These mountains rise everywhere more or less abruptly from the water, forming in places precipitous headlands over 1,000 feet in height . . . (USN 1917: 405).

> The Saguenay is navigable for large vessels nearly to Point Roches, 57 miles from the St. Lawrence and small vessels (sailing craft require the assistance of the flood stream) can ascend to Chicoutimo, 78 miles farther (USN 1917: 406).

> The meeting of the spring ebb streams down the Saguenay and St. Lawrence causes breaking and whirling eddies and riplings, so strong as to interfere with the steerage of a vessel, unless kept at a good speed. These streams, opposed to a heavy northeasterly gale, cause an exceedingly high, cross, and breaking sea, in which no boat could live, and which is even considered dangerous to small vessels (USN 1917: 407).

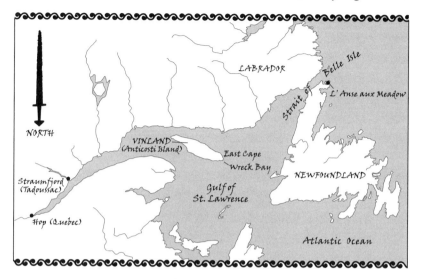

Early European settlements in the Gulf of St. Lawrence were located at L'Anse aux Meadows, Vinland, Hop, and Straumfjord.

Tadoussac . . . is the chief town of Saguenay County and a watering place much frequented by tourists during summer . . . The French explored the Saguenay before the middle of the sixteenth century and Tadoussac soon after became, and remained till the settlement of Canada, their principal post in the St. Lawrence for carrying on their fur trade with the Indians (USN 1917: 409).

Karlsefini established another settlement, Hop, southwest of Straumfjord. He took up residence there, perhaps as far southwest as Quebec. It was at Hop that Indians approached the newcomers with bundles of fine furs to barter. It was also there that settlers' trouble with the Indians began. Karlsefini once even used a bull to frighten away the Indians who seemed about to attack. Eventually, the Indian threat prompted Karlsefini to decide that they could not remain, so those settlers left Hop and returned to Straumfjord. Next, internal strife broke out among the settlers at Straumfjord. Danger of Indian attack again became a concern, so after three years in Vinland, Karlsefini's colony abandoned

Straumfjord and returned to Iceland (Reman 1990: 33–38). While their departure marks the end of recorded colonization efforts, the Karlsefini saga clearly shows that Vinland was settled for several years and was well known to a considerable number of people. Because many residents of Iceland had thus obtained firsthand information about Vinland, it is reasonable to expect that knowledge of Vinland would have become widespread, and that the place name Vinland would be used for the entire St. Lawrence Region.

Approximately 340 years after the Karlsefini expedition, another settlement effort was most likely made in the St. Lawrence region by a group of Norse who abandoned their settlement in Greenland. Helge Ingstad attempted to discover the fate of those Norse Greenlanders who in 1348 abandoned the Western Settlement of Greenland. He concluded that the most likely explanation for their sudden disappearance was that the whole colony had moved to North America (Ingstad 1966: 324 and Ingstad 1969: 94). Ingstad thus accepted as true the 1637 Icelandic account, known as *Gisli Oddsson's Annals*, which told that: "The people of Greenland fell away from the true faith, and after having lost all good customs and true virtue they returned to the American people" (Gjerset 1924: 116) as literally meaning that the Greenlanders sailed to America. Ingstad does not suggest that they settled at L'Anse aux Meadows. Probably the 1348 migration occurred only after some prior exploration and site selection. However, accepting Ingstad's conclusion suggests that the Greenland migrants most likely established their new homes in one or more settlements in the St. Lawrence region, based on the history of its earlier exploration and on the fact that it was the first region they would reach that offered reasonably good conditions for settlement.

A 1348 settlement of Norse from Greenland in Vinland, only 14 years prior to the KRS inscription date of 1362, suggests a possible link between those events. Perhaps a European settlement in the St. Lawrence region encouraged monks to establish a residence nearby. It may be that some of the Norse who had come from Greenland were hired by the Goths (the monks), and were the Northmen who are described in the KRS inscription.

It appears likely that knowledge of Vinland continued in Scandinavia from Leif Erickson's time on. Considering the reference to Vinland written by Adam of Bremen in 1070, there is no reason why such important knowledge would have become lost. The famous Vinland Map, at Yale University, shows the St. Lawrence Gulf. It is very likely that there was intermittent Scandinavian pre-Columbian contact with Vinland during all of the entire medieval period after Leif Erickson. Icelandic accounts written in 1159 and in 1250 confirm that Vinland remained known and was visited in the centuries after the time described in the Sagas (Gjerset 1924: 112). The St. Lawrence Gulf became known to European commercial fishermen at a very early date, and they likely were inclined to keep the source of their wealth secret. Europeans are known to have fished for cod within the gulf for a number of years before the Grand Banks off Newfoundland were discovered (Innis 1940: 11).

Historian Samuel Eliot Morison, in writing about the North American landfalls of Leif Erickson, John Cabot and Jacques Cartier, observed: ". . . what an extraordinary coincidence! The first two Europeans to discover North America, half a millennium apart, hit that vast continent within a few miles of each other; and Jacques Cartier followed suit, 37 years after Cabot" (Morison 1971: 174). Was it a coincidence, or was it evidence that knowledge of the St. Lawrence Gulf region was available to those later explorers? Cartier's account of his first voyage clearly shows that he knew where he was headed when he left France, and that he did not merely happen upon North America. His account states that when he reached the strait (of Belle Isle) he found it blocked by ice, so he landed at a location nearby on the Newfoundland Atlantic seaboard to wait for the strait to open. He obviously knew of the strait so he wasted no effort looking for another entrance. A few days after Cartier had entered the Gulf, he encountered a fishing ship from La Rochelle, France. Nothing in his account indicates that Cartier was surprised to meet a fishing ship from France in the Gulf while on his voyage of discovery.

Everyone knows that the name "Vinland" was coined by Leif Erickson because wild grapes were found there. Jacques Cartier, in his account of his voyages, reports discovering wild grapes in large quantities. While his account of his voyages to the gulf include practically no mention of other plants, he seems to go out of his way to tell of discovering abundant armfuls of wild grapevines at two locations. He first reports finding them opposite the site of modern Quebec, on Ile d'Orleans, which Cartier named "Bachus" because of the grapes. He also reported finding abundant grapevines southwest of Ile d'Orleans when he sailed some distance up the St. Lawrence River. Cartier's odd emphasis on those wild grapevines growing at two places in the St. Lawrence region may have been a tip of his explorer's hat to Leif Erickson. Perhaps it was his way of showing that he had rediscovered Vinland.

Based on these conclusions, when the author of the KRS inscription wrote in 1362 that his group had began their exploration from Vinland, it seems reasonable to conclude that from his perspective he meant a well known place that anyone reading the inscription would be able to identify.

The Route From Vinland

A S FAR AS THE AUTHENTICITY OF THE KRS IS CON-
cerned, we do not need to know exactly which route was
used by the explorers who carved it, only that several
routes were available that could have been used to make the journey described in the inscription. The archaeological and historical
record shows that there were several waterway routes that were
then well established and could have been used. Those routes are
best known as part of Canadian history. To reach Lake Michigan
or Lake Superior from the St. Lawrence the commonly traveled
route was via Canadian rivers into Georgian Bay of Lake Huron.
From Georgian Bay travelers could enter Lake Michigan or Lake
Superior. The ancient Canadian river shortcut routes continue in
use. Archaeologists have established that this waterway route existed for many centuries in pre-Columbian North America for
travel between the St. Lawrence region and the western Great
Lakes. From Lake Michigan or Lake Superior several routes could
have been used to reach the main center of the Dakota Indians at
Lake Mille Lacs in what is now Minnesota. These were the very
same waterway routes followed in the 17th century by European
fur traders, missionaries and explorers, who traveled into the region that is now Minnesota (Morse 1969: 19).

Rather than thinking of the creators of the KRS as furtive
intruders, sneaking into hostile Indian territory, the more likely
situation was that the Europeans were guided on their travel by

For centuries Indians used river shortcuts to travel from the St. Lawrence to the western Great Lakes. The KRS expedition probably took the same routes.

Indians who were familiar with travel and trade in the Great Lakes region. They followed waterway trade routes that had been developed and used by Indians for hundreds of years.

Looking only at U.S. history made it difficult for some to believe that the KRS was authentic because it was found in Minnesota, over a thousand miles from the Atlantic Ocean. Considering the hardships and dangers of travel experienced by the early pioneers, it seemed impossible for any 14th century explorers to have made it as far west as Minnesota. However, the history of 17th century French exploration into the heartland of North America demonstrates that the Canadian river routes would have been equally available to explorers in the 14th century. Modern studies show that Indian use of those routes was more extensive in the 14th century than in later periods because Indian civilization and long distance trade had attained a high level of organization and sophistication in the 13th and 14th centuries, and then disappeared or was greatly reduced for about two centuries prior to the time that post–Columbian Europeans arrived (Gibbon 1974: 129).

While well established waterway routes beginning from Lake Michigan at Green Bay, Wisconsin, and in Illinois could have been used, I believe that the most likely route followed by the 14th century explorers was via Lake Superior, and that they landed somewhere near or at its most western reaches.

The Sea

ONE CAN FIND HUNDREDS OF PUBLISHED ACCOUNTS about Lake Superior that describe it as a "sea." Europeans were astounded by the size of the Great Lakes. Lake Superior, the largest and most dangerous of the five, would certainly have been thought of as a "sea" by the 14th century explorers. After many days of sailing along its southerly shore, there was no better word than "sea" for the explorers to use to describe it. There would have been no particular reason for them to distinguish between fresh and salt water. Therefore when lines 10 through 12 of the KRS inscription state: "We have 10 men by the sea to look after our ships, 14 days' journey from this island" what is meant is that they left their ships at their landing site on Lake Superior, in the care of ten men from their party. The other thirty men of the party (eight Goths and 22 Norrmen) took 14 days to travel from that site to the island camp site where they would later carve the KRS inscription.

Another reason why the word "sea" in the inscription must apply to the Great Lakes is simply because it states they were exploring west from Vinland. If one is traveling west from Vinland, the only large bodies of water west of the eastern seaboard that could be described as "seas" are the Great Lakes. It is also obvious that usage of the word "sea" makes it clear that the explorers had not come up the Mississippi River from the Gulf of Mexico.

The Ships

T HE KRS INSCRIPTION USES THE WORD "SHIPS" which is plural, indicating that the explorers used more than one. While it may have been possible for the explorers to have used two ships that might have been previously used in Atlantic Ocean travel, it seems more likely that the ships they used were built in Vinland, or perhaps in Greenland, and that they were smaller that the usual seagoing Nordic ships. Most likely there were two ships, each carrying 20 men, or perhaps as many as four, each carrying 10 men. The ships would have been light enough so the occupants could portage them for short distances, or tow them when necessary, such as when entering Lake Superior via St. Mary's River, which flows only a short distance from Lake Superior to Lake Michigan. The inscription's statement that the explorers came from Vinland, not Europe, implies that some of the explorers had resided in Vinland for a considerable time, probably several years; and so would have had the time and opportunity to construct medium–sized vessels usable on inland waterways. The ten man vessels would have had about the same capacity as the large freight canoes used on Lake Superior in the fur trade in the 18th century.

Confirmation that such midsize Nordic–style ships were used on inland waterways in the Great Lakes region in the 14th century is given by pictures of them, carved in stone, in the Peterborough (Ontario) Petroglyphs. These Petroglyphs, first unearthed in 1954, have been archaeologically dated to be no later than 1400. Several hundred carvings are found at the Peterborough Provincial Park, including about a dozen carvings of boats that are shown carrying five, six or seven men. The boats resemble Viking ships as they have animal–like prows, a stern steering paddle and, in some cases, a central mast. They are illustrated and described in the book, *Sacred Art of the Algonkians, a Study of the Peterborough Petroglyphs* by Joan M. Vastokas and Romas K. Vastokas.

While the boats carved in stone at Peterborough appear to be similar to Viking–style ships, it is clear that they portray smaller craft with only six or seven men occupying each boat. What the Peterborough Petroglyphs do illustrate, in my opinion, are medieval period boats, made by Europeans in Vinland for use on the Great Lakes waterways. Those rock carvings confirm the existence of boats that were large enough to carry a substantial load on the Great Lakes but small enough to be carried or towed short distances.

Che Journey of Fourteen Days

THE INSCRIPTION STATES THAT IT WAS A 14 DAYS'
journey from the sea where they had left their ships to
the island where the KRS inscription was carved. Ho-
land, in order to make the inscription fit his theory, claimed that a
day's journey referred to an average day's sail of 75 miles. However, it is my conclusion that it is simply a report of a 14 day journey. Typically the European fur traders and explorers landed near
the western end of Lake Superior at the mouth of the Brule River,
then ascended the Brule to a lake which was the source of the St.
Croix River, followed it southerly to the Snake River and then
followed it westerly to the Knife River and to Lake Mille Lacs. By
canoe, that trip took considerably less than 14 days. On the other
hand, the historic route from Green Bay, Wisconsin to the west,
that connected with the Wisconsin River to reach the Mississippi, then headed north on the Mississippi to the St. Croix River,
and on to Knife Lake, would have taken more than 14 days.

The Brule River route, or perhaps some other landing site on
the south shore of Lake Superior, is the most likely when one appreciates that their hosts, the Dakota Indians, did not have birch
bark canoes in the mid-fourteenth century, but instead, used dugouts. It would have been necessary for the Dakotas to assemble
quite a number of dugouts to accommodate thirty visitors. Part of
the route was upstream and part on small streams which may
have then been in low water. Dugouts were far harder to control

From Lake Superior the KRS expedition traveled via the Brule, St. Croix, Snake, and Knife Rivers to reach Lake Mille Lacs.

and were much slower than canoes. It would have been necessary to take time to hunt or fish for food to feed the group. Probably the monks felt obliged to stop for frequent prayers, and perhaps some of the explorers were ill. At any rate there are many reasons why it would have been a slow trip.

While the route was routine and well-known to the Dakota Indians who led the party, it would have been very difficult for the visitors to attempt to describe it considering the various streams and lakes and directions of travel. The best they could do was to keep track of the number of days. Keeping a record of the day was very important to the monks, so that they could observe Sunday and holy days. Considering all the many possible difficulties, it seems reasonable to conclude that the 14 days' journey reported in the KRS applies to the travel of the explorers from Lake Superior to Knife Lake.

The Dakotas at Mille Lacs

MY BELIEF THAT THE PLACE IDENTIFIED IN THE inscription as being by "two skerries," refers to the southerly shore area of Lake Mille Lacs, Minnesota, and that the island where the inscription was carved and left standing was in Knife Lake, in Kanabec county, Minnesota, rests upon significant circumstantial evidence including data from history, geography and geology.

While most of the linkage between the Dakota Indians and the KRS will be described in Part II of this book, at this point it is necessary to establish the basic historical facts that in the 14th century all of what is now Minnesota and western Wisconsin was Dakota Indian territory, and in that whole region, the center for Dakota leadership and population (their capital, so to speak) was located in the Lake Mille Lacs and Knife Lake area. Lake Mille Lacs was, and is, a very large and productive lake. William Warren described its wonders over 150 years ago concluding: "... there is not a spot in the northwest which an Indian would sooner choose as a home and dwelling place, than Mille Lacs" (Warren 1885: 156). The Dakota Indians made it their largest and leading center for that same reason. Minnesota's regional historians including, Edward Neill, J. V. Brower, N. H. Winchell, and Theodore Blegen, all agreed that Lake Mille Lacs and the Knife Lake area were the central location of the Dakota Indians for many centuries, until about 1750.

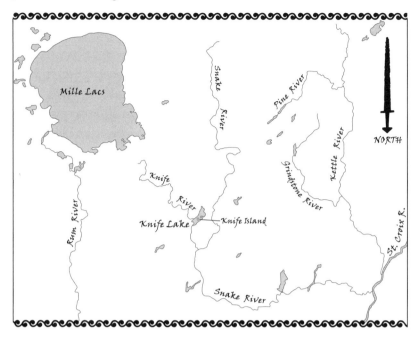

Knife Island in Knife Lake was the site where the KRS was carved.

Dakota Indian history also confirms that fact. Probably the most reliable account of Dakota Indian history taken from Dakota sources was recorded by James R. Walker in the early 20th century, on the Pine Ridge Reservation in South Dakota. Walker's research makes it clear that the Dakota memory of their past at Lake Mille Lacs and Knife Lake continued to be strong, even though about 150 years had passed since they had left that region (Walker 1982: 13–18). "They believed that the Mysterious Lake (Lake Mille Lacs) was the center of the world . . ." (Walker 1982: 16). It is remarkable that Dakota oral history retained that memory for so long considering that they had moved many times since, had divided into several council fires or groups, and had endured many hardships and military assaults. By the 20th century the Dakota Indians had been living on the Great Plains for generations and had developed a new culture focused on the horse and buffalo. Plains life differed a great deal from their former woodland society centered at Lake Mille Lacs, nevertheless their new culture had not erased the traditions that originated in the forests near Lake Mille Lacs.

The geographical circumstances and historical records compel the conclusion that 14th century Europeans following the Great Lakes waterway to the western end of Lake Superior, necessarily would have arrived in the domain of the Dakota Indians. Assuming a cordial contact, based on mutual curiousity, mutual respect for the strength and weapons each carried, and trade possibilities, we can assume that the Dakota hosts would have escorted the visitors to their main center in the Lake Mille Lacs area, just as they did in the 17th century when various parties led by French explorers suddenly appeared at the westerly end of Lake Superior. A fourteenth century contact probably would not have differed greatly from one which took place in the 17th century, and so it seems reasonable to look to the history of that century, where several written accounts of such contact exist. More details of the 17th century contacts will be found in the Dakota section of this book.

The Two Skerries of
Lake Mille Lacs

T HE WORD "SKERRY" IN THE KRS INSCRIPTION,
means a rocky islet. It indicates more than a single rock,
but not a habitable site, which would be called an island.
Because the KRS inscription uses both terms, "skerry" and "island," it is clear that the author distinguished between those
terms, and his careful choice of terms confirms that his use of
"skerry," described a rocky islet. In contrast, he used the word "island" to describe the place where the KRS was carved, presumably the island where the explorers had made their main camp.

The author of the KRS inscription wished to identify the location of the camp where his ten comrades had died, but had no
place name, so he chose the two skerries as landmarks and reference points. It never occurred to the author that the rune stone
would be moved. The two skerries would have seemed like good
choices to use as landmarks because they were unusual features.
The author knew that one day's journey north from their island in
Knife Lake brought one to the south shore of Lake Mille Lacs,
and that the two boulder islets located in the south part of Lake
Mille Lacs were clearly visible from that shore. Those circumstances led the KRS author to think that someone reading the inscription would be able to easily identify the site, because the two
skerries were obviously unusual local features. They still are. The
reference to "two skerries," applies quite uniquely to the southerly
shore of Lake Mille Lacs. The lake is huge, having about 207

Spirit Island in Lake Mille Lacs, 1929.
Spirit Island is the larger and most westerly of the two large boulder islands
which are the two "skerries" used as landmarks in the KRS inscription.
Photographic postcard from the author's collection.

square miles of water area, and is more or less round in shape.
From the southerly shore two small boulder islets can be seen.
The islets are only rock, consisting of the large heavy boulders
that remained after all finer material had been washed away by
the high waves that often sweep across the lake's broad expanse.
Those boulder islets are sufficiently unusual features, that they
merit particular mention and pictures in popular books on Minnesota geology (Schwartz and Thiel 1963: 265, 267). The islets are
now named Spirit Island and Hennepin Island.

In prior considerations of the route of the explorers and the location of the places referred to, the assumption was that a massacre had occurred, followed by the second assumption that the
explorers had then fled to the site where they carved the inscription, one day's journey south of the massacre site. To the contrary,
my hypothesis is that the explorers, by following the ancient route
west from the St. Croix and the Snake River to Knife River, had

reached their main camp at Knife Lake on their arrival in the area. Probably some days later they had been guided from that camp by the Dakota one day's journey north to Lake Mille Lacs where they set up their fishing camp. Lake Mille Lacs had abundant quantities of fish so presumably the Dakotas were assisting them in catching a large supply. Then, after the 10 men were found dead, the explorers had retraced their route southerly one day's journey to their main camp at Knife Lake. Very likely many days passed before they came up with the idea of carving a rune stone to tell of the deaths of their comrades and to mark the extent of their exploration. An unusual feature of the inscription tends to support this hypothesis. The reference to the two skerries in the KRS inscription fails to include a word to describe the body of water in which they were located; requiring translators to supply the word "lake" from the context. Why was the word "lake" omitted? The Goths must have had a word for lake. Again, we must look to the perspective of the author. From the south shore, looking north, Lake Mille Lacs is so large that its northerly shore cannot be seen. It looks like a "sea." Was it really a lake or another sea like Lake Superior? Because the author had approached Mille Lacs from the south, he had no opportunity to learn the extent of its waters and so he would have been uncertain what word should be used to describe it. To avoid error, he chose to rely only upon a reference to the two skerries as landmarks.

Graywacke and Calcite

NE WAY TO KNOW THAT YOU ARE ON THE RIGHT track in solving a puzzle is when you find unexpected new information that supports your hypothesis. In this case it was learning that graywacke rock, with the same characteristics as that of the KRS, was a significant component of the glacial deposits found over the entire south shore area of Lake Mille Lacs and Knife Lake region. That area is a massive glacial moraine known as the Superior Lobe, which gets its name from the fact that it is material removed from the Lake Superior area by glacial action. When the glaciers that once covered most of Minnesota and Wisconsin moved slowly southward, the ice, which was several miles thick, gouged deeply into the old land surface, and carried away many feet of rock and soil. That material was then carried along with the glacial ice until the glacier melted and the rock and other soil it was carrying was deposited. Geologists have in some instances been able to trace the movements of the glaciers by identifying rock found in the drift as having originated from upstream rock formations that were only partially removed by the glacier. That is the case with the Superior Lobe.

Graywacke, from which the KRS was made, is a very hard black rock, very similar to slate, except that graywacke is more massive in structure, while slate occurs in thinner layers and is more brittle. An unusual aspect of the graywacke boulder used to create the KRS is that another mineral, calcite, adheres to a portion of the graywacke surface on the front. Part of the KRS inscription was carved into that calcite concretion.

The Superior Lobe contains large amounts of graywacke rock that glaciers carved out of a huge formation known as the Thomson formation. One of the unusual aspects of the graywacke found in the Thomson formation is that it was regularly interlaced with calcite intrusions, which are clearly visible in the lower parts of the Thomson formation that remained untouched by the glacier. The presence of calcite adhering to graywacke on the KRS points to its origin in some part of the Thomson formation that was removed by the glacier and later deposited in the Superior Lobe, which as previously noted, comprises the whole southern shore region of Lake Mille Lacs and the Knife Lake area.

To better understand this issue, it is helpful to review some of the early KRS research. In 1910, the Minnesota Historical Society sought the help of a blue ribbon committee of experts that was charged with the responsibility of making a recommendation to the society respecting the authenticity or the fraudulent origin of the Kensington Rune Stone and its inscription. The committee report was published in Volume 15 of *The Minnesota Historical Society Collections*. The committee unanimously adopted a favorable opinion of the authenticity of the Kensington rune stone, with the proviso that the report was not expected to terminate the investigation, but to show the present belief of its members.

The most prominent committee member was Prof. N. H. Winchell, who wrote much of its report. He was then 70 years old. He had graduated from the University of Michigan in 1866 and worked on geological surveys in Michigan and Ohio until becoming the Minnesota State Geologist in 1872. He published 24 volumes of annual reports during his tenure, and between 1884 and 1901 published a comprehensive survey of Minnesota Geology in six large volumes. He was chief editor of the *American Geologist*, Minneapolis, which issued 36 volumes from 1888 to 1905. He also served as a professor of mineralogy and geology at the University of Minnesota. His versatility in scholarship is illus-

trated by the fact today he is mainly remembered as the chief author of *The Aborigines of Minnesota*, a 761 page book, published in
1911, that still stands as the most comprehensive work on Minnesota's Indian history. While engaged in the KRS investigation,
Winchell made three trips to the Kensington area and had the
KRS available for study at the state historical society for over a
year. He described the KRS in his report to the Minnesota Historical Society, as follows:

> The extreme length of the Rune Stone is 36 inches, the
> width across the face 15 inches, the thickness 5 and 1/2
> inches, and its weight is about 230 pounds. It is of gray-
> wacke, but its shape and dark color suggest that it is trap. Its
> flat surfaces and angular jointage are due apparently to long
> continued heating and slow cooling in contact, or near con-
> tact, with igneous rocks. On its inscribed face is a layer of
> calcite covering a part of the area in which the inscription
> was engraved. This calcite was deposited in a jointage-
> opening, probably when the rock was in its native place; and
> it has been revealed by the removal of an adjoining parallel
> mass, the joint plane itself causing the even face on which
> the engraving was made. The reverse of the inscribed side is
> not so regular and has evidently been through the rough ex-
> periences of glacial action, since it bears a number of dis-
> tinct glacial striae (Winchell 1915: 225).

It seems clear from Winchell's descriptions that the KRS inscription was carved into a fresh cut, after a stone mason had divided the boulder by splitting it along the seam of calcite intrusion which existed in the original larger graywacke boulder.
Visual inspection of the KRS clearly shows chisel marks on the
right side as you face the inscription face, indicating that the
larger graywacke boulder was split along the line of chisel marks,
resulting in an essentially flat surface as the boulder divided along
the calcite intrusion. Apparently most of the calcite intrusion
adhered to the side which was removed and discarded, leaving

only part of the surface used for the inscription still covered with calcite. In contrast, the rear of the stone shows no sign of masonry work, but clearly shows long scratches (striae) from glacial action, as Winchell noted.

Winchell also observed that the side, or edge, of the KRS that was inscribed with lines 9 through 12 had been hammered into a more level surface before the inscription was carved. Splitting the boulder and leveling one edge reflect the work of a skilled and experienced stone mason. There is no evidence that Ohman, nor any of his friends, ever possessed or practiced those skills.

Knowing that the boulder was split along the calcite intrusion seam, and that the inscription was carved into the freshly exposed surface also means that if it was carved at the discovery site, then we should expect to find the other part, or half, of the boulder that was separated when the stone was split. That site has been closely studied and no other graywacke pieces that might have been cut away from the KRS have ever been reported. The absence of waste graywacke material at the discovery site is another reason to conclude that the KRS was carved elsewhere.

Graywacke is a sedimentary rock, usually very old, which has been subjected to great pressure, and has a hardness next to granite. One of best known and largest deposits of graywacke in the Minnesota area comprises a major part of the Thomson Formation, which occurs in the Lake Superior area. The Thomson Formation is huge and outcrops at various locations over an area of some 500 square miles. Estimates of its thickness range from 3,000 to as much as 20,000 feet (Sims and Morey 1972: 246). A very significant characteristic of the massive quantity of graywacke rock found in the Thomson formation is that it is interlaced with regular calcium carbonate (calcite) concretions throughout the formation (Schwartz 1949: 20–1).

While the Thomson formation that still exists is very large, it is only the remnant, the lower level, of a much larger formation cut down to its present level by glacial action. As noted, the upper portion of the Thomson graywacke was removed and transported southwesterly where, when the glacial ice melted, it eventually become a major component of the glacial drift known as the Superior Lobe. Winchell's description of the reverse side of the Kensington stone was that it had "a number of distinct glacial striae" which confirms that the KRS graywacke boulder had been subjected to glacial transportation, proving that it came out of the glacial drift, rather than being a stone that had been quarried from a bed of graywacke, such as exists in the remaining Thomson formation.

The geological history of the Superior Lobe moraine has been studied and written about by several geologists, making it probably the most clearly identified glacial deposit in Minnesota. It is the presence of that moraine, forming something of a container, that is responsible for the existence of Lake Mille Lacs. The Superior Lobe moraine also extends southerly from Lake Mille Lacs for many miles, and includes the Knife Lake area (Bray 1977: 71; Sims and Morey 1972: 525, 530–1; Wright 1990: 6; Ojakangas and Matsch 1982: 213). The geological history of the Superior Lobe moraine means that many boulders of graywacke with calcite concretions, were removed from somewhere in the Thomson formation and ended up as part of the glacial drift. It is my conclusion that, in 1362, one of them was selected by the creators of the KRS. Recently, several investigators, including Barry Hanson and Scott Wolter, have been studying the mineral composition of the KRS and have announced tentative findings which, I believe, are consistent with my hypothesis that the KRS was made from a graywacke boulder found in the Superior Lobe moraine (Hanson and Wolter 2000).

The KRS and the Thomson graywacke are both characterized by extensive jointing, which means that the rock bed is divided by regular lines of separation that divide the rocks into parallel sections. In the Thomson graywacke the joint separations are even about the same width as those of the KRS. It may well be the case that the sides of the KRS were joint separations. It would appear that the authors of the KRS inscription began by selecting a graywacke boulder that had fairly regular parallel sides caused by jointing. Then they split the boulder along a calcite intrusion which was perpendicular to the jointed sides, which exposed a fresh and fairly flat surface where the main inscription was carved. Probably the stone masons trimmed the top and bottom to create a more rectangular shape, and hammered the left side smooth to receive the inscription on that side, while the reverse side of the KRS was left untouched and still shows evidence of the glacial scars. It's possible that the explorers cut several boulders before obtaining what they needed. So, if their work site can be found, it may be identifiable from waste from old stone cutting when the KRS was shaped, as well as from possible other stone cutting. One would also hope that medieval artifacts would be discovered to confirm the site.

A graywacke artifact, which may be relevant to the KRS, was found a century ago at Lake Mille Lacs. It was identified as an Indian scraper, and was found there by J. V. Brower, who described it as a large chipped flake, made from a boulder spall (Brower and Bushnell 1900: Plate III in Vol. 3). Winchell included the same illustration in *The Aborigines of Minnesota* and added the information that it was a "giant flake of graywacke" (Winchell 1911: 462). Winchell seemed to have been particularly interested in the scraper, as he wrote:

> The largest flake in the Brower collection is represented by plate IV (of scrapers, etc). It is of fine-grained graywacke and shows on the flat surface, at the broader end, a series of fracture indulations running from the end diagonally across the face, indicating the point where the ictus was applied . . . The size of the spall itself demonstrates that the flaking was done by some powerful instrument in the hands of a powerful man. This spall is 7 7/8 inches by 3 inches. One edge is slightly broken, as if by usage, but otherwise the flake is fresh. Perhaps the only tool the aboriginal man had for forming flakes of this size was a stone

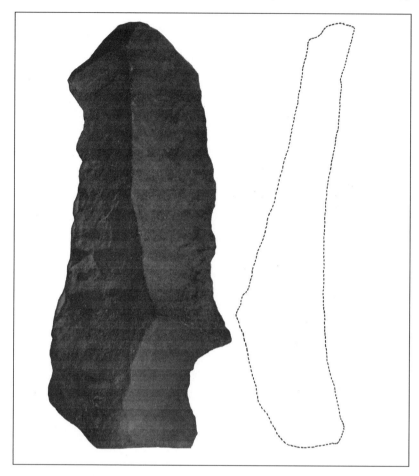

Graywacke Flake.
This large chipped flake may once have been part of the Kensington Rune
Stone. It was found at Nichols Bay, on Lake Mille Lacs, Minnesota.
From J. V. Brower and D. T. Bushnell, *Mille Lac* (1900), Plate III.

hammer, but to a white man it appears necessary to use a
heavy steel maul which had a firm angular face, or a
chisel . . . (Winchell 1911: 463).

Winchell's question about how the graywacke scraper could
have been cut from a larger rock is resolved once we appreciate
that European stone masons, using iron tools of their craft, were

working in stone during their 14th century contact with the Dakota Indians in the Mille Lacs area. One tantalizing possibility is that the graywacke scraper found by Brower may have been cut from the bottom of the KRS itself. Examination shows that the bottom of the KRS was shaped into a more pointed base, to facilitate its being placed in the ground. The shape of the graywacke scraper found by Brower looks as if it may have been cut from the KRS as part of that work. Perhaps the precise mineral content of the two examples of graywacke can be analyzed to determine if the flake was once part of the KRS boulder.

Part of Winchell's study of the KRS also included a field survey of the discovery site area in Douglas county. He reported that:

> The topography of Mr. Ohman's farm and the adjoining country is morainic, the elevations rising sometimes somewhat abruptly to the height of fifty or seventy-five feet, or even a hundred feet, above the adjoining lowlands. The material of the drift is clay of a limonitic yellow color, but at a depth of fifteen to twenty feet this clay is blue. There are very few boulders in the clay, yet on the tops of some of the drift hills granitic and other boulders are numerous, and sometimes they are found in numbers near the bases of the hills and in the swamps. They are sometimes large and conspicuous, and frequently have been gathered into heaps in the fields. About seventy-five in a hundred of the boulders are of granite; about five in a hundred are of limestone; about five in a hundred are of gabbro or of gabbroid rocks; five in a hundred are of Keewatin greenstone, including Ogishke conglomerate; about five in a hundred are of dark nondescript rock, sometimes quartzose; and the other five in a hundred may be compared with the rock of the rune stone, being some of the various forms of graywacke (Winchell 1915: 24).

We must assume that if Winchell had found any boulders of graywacke with calcite concretions or intrusions, he would have reported it. However, he only reports finding a few graywacke rocks, which "may be compared with the rock of the rune stone, being some of the various forms of graywacke." Obviously he was looking for boulders like the one used to create the KRS, but he never claimed to have found any. Nor has anyone else ever reported finding any graywacke boulders with calcite concretions similar to the KRS in the discovery area. The absence of similar graywacke boulders with calcite concretions or intrusions indicates that the boulder used to make the KRS was not one native to the glacial drift in the region where the KRS was found; and supports the idea that the KRS was brought to its burial site from elsewhere.

Undoubtedly Winchell was a leading member of the committee that unanimously decided that the KRS was authentic. Experts who evaluate questioned documents, old paintings and collectable objects, develop a sense or a "feel" for the genuine as compared to the fake. To such experts an object looks right, or it doesn't. Winchell, by 1910, had worked with more artifacts and geological issues in Minnesota than anyone else who has ever considered the KRS. It was his opinion that the KRS was authentic, and in my view, his judgment was sound.

Another major issue bearing on the age of the KRS inscription arises because the calcite in which part of the inscription was carved is very susceptible to erosion by weathering. It is my hypothesis that the KRS was protected from weathering because soon after the explorers left the area, the Dakota Indians covered it, probably with hides, to restrain its supposed supernatural power. It probably remained covered for most of the approximately 500 year period that it remained in Dakota possession, until they finally buried it near Kensington, where the calcite was protected by the soil that covered it. That is how the calcite survived. It is interesting to review Winchell's comments on the calcite issue. He wrote:

It is plain that the calcite deposit that covers a part of it was formed in a joint-opening before the stone was separated from its neighbor, and that it has had approximately as long direct exposure to the elements as the rest of that surface. It is evident that either the calcite has but recently been exposed or has been protected from the weather . . . In short, there is no possible natural way to preserve that calcite scale from general disintegration for 548 years except to bury it beneath the surface. If it was not thus buried and still is intact, it must have been exposed and the inscription must have been made less than a hundred years ago, and probably less than thirty years ago (Winchell 1915: 235–6).

Winchell and the committee's unanimous conclusion that the inscription was authentic, clearly, necessarily, rested on their assumption that the calcite had been protected from weathering.

Stone Carving Monks

BEFORE REVIEWING THE MANY REASONS WHY IT IS most likely that the KRS was carved by 14th century monks of the Roman Catholic Church, one clue that points to Cistercian monks as its author stands out and merits first mention. It is the use of AVM, Ave Maria, in the inscription. That well-known usage is not as ancient as one might suppose. Adriaan H. Bredero, in his book, *Christendom and Christianity in the Middle Ages*, states that the significant role of the Virgin Mary in the Roman Catholic Church developed from visions of Cistercian monks in 1260, and that, "The Ave Maria became a popular prayer in Cistercian circles, which led to the gradual development of the rosary, though the term rosary dates only from the fifteenth century" (Bredero 1994: 339). Thus the use of AVM in the KRS inscription of 1362 is an early usage pointing to Cistercian authorship or influence.

The KRS was a medieval inscription so we must view it from the perspective of that period. This means that while it is possible to identify many events in Scandinavian history in the period shortly prior to 1362 that might have prompted the explorers who carved the KRS to undertake their travel and exploration, we must also acknowledge the possibility that the explorers' motives came from reasons that we normally would not see as logical, such as in response to a vision, or some other spiritual quest.

Modern historians emphasize that the medieval period differs from our modern era to a much greater extent than modern man can readily imagine. For example, Carolly Erickson in her book, *The Medieval Vision*, begins by writing how her understanding of the medieval period evolved during her research, as the more she probed the more she appreciated how differently life and the world were perceived then compared to today (Erickson 1976: v). In her first chapter titled "The Enchanted World," she described a late thirteenth century manuscript which tells the story of a journey by three monks who set out to find the place where heaven and earth meet. Their tale includes obvious pure fancy, which was combined with an account that appears to describe a real physical journey. Erickson described medieval understanding as "an enchanted world in which the boundaries of imagination and of actuality are constantly shifting" (Erickson 1976: 5). In respect to geography she concluded "readiness to believe that real lands underlay geographical legends spurred an exploratory mentality . . ." (Erickson 1976: 7). She also describes the great significance that was given to visions in the medieval period, commenting: "We who assign such things to the fringes of reality cannot easily recognize the awesome import of visions for people who set them at its center" (Erickson 1976: 36).

In the 14th century, St. Bridget of Sweden, at about age 40, after the death of her husband, began having religious visions that were recorded by her confessors. These visions prompted the King of Sweden to grant her the royal estate of Vadstena in 1346. Then, in response to more visions, she left Sweden for Rome, where she lived for the rest of her life, and continued to have visions. In describing medieval acceptance of St. Bridget's visions, Swedish historian Ingvar Anderson commented: "It would not have occurred to any medieval man or woman to doubt the authenticity of these visions" (Anderson 1956: 57).

Several factors narrow the search for the author of the KRS inscription. He had to have been one of the very few people who could travel to remote and little known places, and one of the few who was sufficiently literate to draft the inscription, and also one of a very small number who was skilled enough in stone working to enable him to prepare or shape the KRS and then carve its inscription. He identified himself as a Goth. Those factors narrow the search to the monastic world of the Roman Catholic Church and Gotland.

In the 14th century individual travel was rare and dangerous, literacy was rare outside of the Church, and stone working and stone carving skills were very limited. The most dominant and unified power in Europe was the Roman Catholic Church, and it had held that power for centuries. The Roman Catholic Church was then organized much as today with Bishops in charge of certain territories. Bishops reported to Archbishops who reported to Cardinals and thence to the Pope. The Bishop was a powerful figure. However, outside that structure, monastic orders had their own leadership, that was independent of the Bishops and sometimes in conflict with them. Monastic orders in some cases were founded by reformers dedicated to a simple God–centered life. Monastic orders attracted many candidates and were usually self-supporting, and often growing rich when wealthy individuals were pursuaded to leave their property to the order, so that they might earn favor with God. As monastic orders prospered, their original high purpose sometimes was lost and monks hired workers to do the manual labor and lived comfortably on the income. The loss of zeal by mature orders sometimes motivated new reformers to found new orders with fresh dedication. Some monastic groups were founded for specific purposes, such as the Templars, the Teutonic Knights, the Knights of Malta, and the Hospitallers. A major aspect of the monastic world was that each order, to a considerable degree, was independent and could chart its own mission and lifestyle. One result of that independence was that monastic groups were sometimes free to travel and relocate as they chose; and that opportunity, which was rare in the 14th century, could have provided the freedom and the idea for the monks who carved the KRS to sail to Vinland. The Cistercian monastic movement expanded in the 13th century as monks left comfortable monasteries and relocated in isolated small groups in remote frontier regions (Cantor 1993: 248). They prospered, so by the 14th century many of those new frontier sites had become rich and comfortable. Realizing that irony, perhaps a group of dedicated Cistercians opted to begin again in Vinland.

The monastic world attracted many of the most capable and intelligent men of the time. The monasteries were islands of literacy in a mostly illiterate world and the copying of books was nearly exclusively in their hands. By the time of the Black Death in the mid-14th century the monastic movement had grown to huge numbers, with many different orders in various stages of growth and decline. It is not difficult to think that somewhere out of that rich mixture of talented men, one group of monks sailed to Vinland, and eventually became the explorers who created the KRS.

Local, free lance monastic orders were also common in the medieval period—often starting with an abbot and 12 monks, representing Christ and his 12 Apostles (Heer 1961: 41). Large new monastic orders in the 12th century included the Cistercian and the Premonstratensian monks who were skilled in stone work and who built structures of high quality which are still standing. By 1270 the Cistercians had 671 abbeys in Western Europe (Heer 1961: 43). One of the functions of some monastic orders, including the Cistercians, was to carry the faith to new unchurched territory. A missionary purpose, the unsettled warfare of the 14th century, and the terror of the Black Death, were all good reasons why a group of monks may have elected to travel to Vinland.

Today it is difficult to comprehend how completely the church dominated nearly all of life in Western Europe in the 14th century. The Church exercised power that today is reserved to the State in matters of criminal law and punishment. Bishops maintained private armies. Heretics were burned at the stake. The Church's wishes were enforced by physical force including torture and execution. Friedrich Heer, Professor of the History of Ideas at the University of Vienna, described the basis for the power of the Church in the medieval period in his book, *The Medieval*

World: Europe 1100–1350. Heer wrote that the medieval Roman Catholic Church fostered the notion that it could protect people from the powers and perils of the natural world that seemed ready to strike one down at any time. Acceptance of this idea by the people gave the Church practically unchallenged power (Heer 1961: 39). Heer noted that about the only limitation on the exercise of power of the Church was the more or less inherently peaceful nature of Christian teachings, plus the fact that strict control was often difficult because of the problems of communication in the medieval period. Many lived in relative isolation that tended to leave matters in the hands of local church authorities (Heer 1961: 40).

An example of the long-range reach of the Roman Catholic Church in this period, probably more challenging than a voyage to Vinland, is reported in Volume III of *A History of the Crusades.* Writing on the 14th century Roman Catholic Church in China, Aziz S. Atiya noted that by 1305 two churches had been built at Khanbaliq (now Bejing) and five thousand had been baptized. However, Church presence in medieval China ended when its leader, James of Florence, was murdered in 1362 (Atiya 1975: 14). It is an interesting coincidence that James of Florence was killed in Cathay in 1362, the same year as the date on the KRS.

The famous Vinland Map was once bound together with a book about travel in Asia, presumably because the individual who compiled the book erroneously assumed that Vinland was the Eastern Shore of Asia. The explorers who carved the Kensington inscription may also have made that same assumption about Vinland. In 1362 the New World was unknown as such. Based on the known world, the explorers who carved the KRS had to think that they were in Asia. Therefore, they would have expected that by going west from Vinland, they would reach Cathay and Khanbaliq. That idea may have been re-enforced in their minds if Indians in Vinland told them about great cities in the west, particularly Cahokia which was then a thriving city of some 25,000 people, located on the east bank of the Mississippi (opposite present-day

St. Louis, Missouri). In 1362, a city with a population of 25,000 would have ranked among the largest cities in the world, and the monks could well assume it was Khanbaliq. Or like Coronado in 1540, the monks may have been lured inland by reports of great cities, rich in gold, in the west.

When the KRS was discovered, anti-American feeling in Scandinavia had grown strong because of the major loss of their youthful population to the United States, and so interest in anything American was discouraged. Furthermore, the KRS could expect only scant acceptance from Scandinavian historians because most were loath to acknowledge anything positive that was attributable to what one Swedish historian, Anders Fryxell, described as, "the Catholic Period." This perspective can be seen from his description of convent life at Vadstena: "It is also very certain that the other vows of their order were at that time not better kept; they required greater self-denial and strength than men usually possess, and often exacted empty and useless exercises; so that they were in the end despised, and here, as in most other convents, manifold sins and vices were hidden under a veil of hypocrisy and devotion" (Fryxell 1844: 277). Scandinavia's negative attitude towards the Roman Catholic Church continues, according to James France, author of *The Cistercians in Scandinavia*, wherein he observed: "… Scandinavians are still prone to view the medieval period, of which the monastic idea is seen as thoroughly representative, as an unfortunate interlude between the heroic Viking past and the enlightenment of the modern age with its beginning at the Reformation" (France 1992: xiv).

A basic error in identifying the creators of the KRS has been the assumption that the terms—Goths and Norrmen—used in the inscription, meant Swedes and Norwegians. That twentieth century assumption would not have been the understanding of the author of the inscription. In the fourteenth century the Goths were a separate people, and were not Swedes. The Goths living in Sweden have now become Swedes, and parts of what was once the language of the Goths have been incorporated into the Swedish language. However, in 1362, a Goth would have identified himself as a Goth in order to distinguish his ethnicity from others, including Swedes. If it had been a group of Swedes, the inscription would have said so. In 1785, over four hundred years later, Swedish King Gustav III, continued to recognize the multiple ethnic origins of the Swedish population by identifying himself as "King of Sweden, the Goths and the Wends" in Royal decrees.

Likewise, it is far from certain that the term "Norrmen" as used in the inscription, means Norwegian, as has been assumed by modern writers. More likely, from the perspectives of the Goths of 1362, all Scandinavians were "Norrmen," meaning, northern men. The word "Viking" referred to all Scandinavians. When the medieval English prayed, "from the fury of the Northmen deliver us," they were not only worried about Norwegians—they knew that Viking raiders came from many Scandinavian areas.

Hakon Melberg, in his book, *Origin of the Scandinavian Nations and Languages,* makes the point that people are often named by their neighbors, not by themselves. He cites as an example of that practice the name, Norway, which he states was a directional name (Northway) used by those who lived to the south (Melberg 1949: 412). He quotes from Adam of Bremen, who wrote that the Danes and Swedes and other peoples who lived beyond Denmark were all called "Nortmanni," and that the North Germanic term for Scandinavians was "Nordmenn" (Melberg 1949: 414–5). Therefore, from the perspective of a Goth in 1362, it seems likely that the name "Norrmen," would be used to describe any Scandinavian, whether Dane, Swede or Norwegian, or a combination; and that term would also have been used to identify the descendants of the Norse who had then lived in Iceland or Greenland for many generations, and would also have been applied to Scandinavians who then may have resided in Vinland.

Gotland, the home of the Goths, was a rich and important commercial center during the medieval period, and its principal city, Visby, was one of the great cities of medieval Europe. Historian Friedrich Heer wrote: "... today Visby is a ghost town, its old

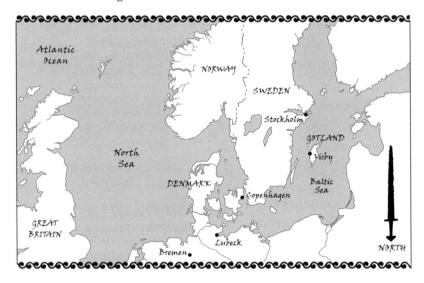

The island of Gotland in the Baltic Sea where the KRS monks may once have lived.

churches and ruins a reminder that medieval north-eastern Europe had its period of splendour" (Heer 1961: 65). Gotland's island location in the Baltic Sea made it a natural trading crossroads. German traders used Gotland as their doorway to trade with the rest of Scandinavia, the Baltic States area and Russia. Visby was the home for The United Gotland Travellers of the Holy Roman Empire, a predecessor of the Hanseatic League. Heer also wrote:

> Gotland was a clearinghouse in artistic matters as well, importing Westphalian architectural styles. Russian furs made the Germans the masters of the Baltic. Furs were then believed to be possessed of magical powers, and in the Middle Ages a luxury fur was the supreme mark of prestige in the matter of dress (Heer 1961: 65).

By the mid–14th century, many Roman Catholic European monasteries, including the Cistercians, had become very rich and owned various commercial enterprises. It is quite possible that monks from Gotland sailed to Vinland to arrange a fur trading enterprise.

In *A Survey of Swedish Art* Carl G. Laurin wrote: "Without doubt, Gotland was . . . where the art of building attained its highest development during the Middle Ages. The golden period falls in the thirteenth and fourteenth centuries, and many a stately church sprang up . . . behind the defiant city wall . . ." (Laurin 1922: 40). "Gotland belonged to the bishopric of Linkoping, and with the help of the Gotlanders, who were skilled in stone work, one of the most stately cathedrals of the land was erected in the city of Linkoping. It is said to have been begun shortly after the year 1200, and the construction went on during the whole of the thirteenth century, the first half of the fourteenth—the work was interrupted by the Great Plague—and the fifteenth century" (Laurin 1922: 45). Except for Gotland, stone masons in Scandinavia were scarce. Norway is well known for its medieval Stave Churches, which were made from wood, not stone. The Nicolai Church, at Gran, Norway, is one of the few medieval stone churches built in Norway, and according to Vatican records, it was a 20-year project, and because Norwegian stonemasons were not available, it was erected by English stonemasons. They apparently taught local workers the craft because the second church, built adjacent to the first, was done by local stone masons (Helmen n.d.: 8).

The language of medieval Gotland was Gotlandic, not Swedish. In his history of the island, historian Arthur Spencer describes the Gotlandic language as follows:

> The old language sounds harsh and primitive. As a famous Swedish actor said: 'It has a singular smack of blood and heathendom.' It uses many gutturals and broad diphthongs, like Anglo-Saxon or Icelandic. Individual words are often clearly related to other Germanic languages in an interesting but curiously indiscriminate manner; and on the whole to Icelandic, Gothic, Old Norse or Old German rather than to Swedish (Spencer 1974: 148).

Gotlandic and Swedish were significantly different to warrant publishing a Gotlandic-Swedish dictionary in 1918 (Spencer 1974:

148). Therefore it seems clear that a native of Gotland in the 14th century learned a language that had evolved at the crossroads of the Baltic, that had been impacted throughout the Viking era by many other contacts, and also enriched by transient churchmen and merchant activity. It was not a language in which one could expect uniformity. It should be clear that any modern linguist who attempts to evaluate the language that was used in the KRS inscription in 1362, by one particular well traveled monk, who was a native of Gotland, must look to Gotlandic usages of language and runes, and also must appreciate the possibility of new terms and phrases that might have been learned by travel elsewhere, or acquired from those who had visited or moved to Gotland from distant places.

Paul B. Du Chaillu, a well-known 19th century travel writer, visited Gotland and wrote of seeing memorial stones with runic texts dated in the 14th and 15th centuries (Du Chaillu 1882: 305). His report confirms that usage of runes in stone inscriptions continued much later on Gotland than elsewhere in Scandinavia.

Historian Franklin D. Scott notes that churches on the Swedish mainland were usually constructed of wood, while there were some 90 churches on Gotland built of stone; and that the stone walls around Visby, built prior to 1361, totaled two and one-half miles in length and had 55 large defensive towers (Scott 1977: 74). Historian Louis J. Lekai wrote that the Cistercian Abbey of Gutvalla on Gotland possessed rich agricultural lands in Estonia and that "Its busy commercial activity presupposes also the maintenance of a considerable fleet" (Lekai 1953: 219). There can be no doubt that the stone mason's craft was a major activity on Gotland. Medieval Gotland had many small seaports which could accommodate craft up to about 60 feet in length with a shallow draft (Scott 1977: 74). Small seaports would easily accommodate a small craft leaving Gotland with a group of monks.

The 27th of July, 1361, is a date still remembered on Gotland as their day of infamy, because it was the date of their great defeat at the hands of King Valdemar Atterdag of Denmark when the

Gotlanders who had assembled to defend Visby were all slaughtered by Valdemar's forces. Gotland was never again to play a major independent role in Scandinavia. The victorious Valdemar added "King of the Goths" to his title. The proximity of the Danish conquest in July, 1361, and the 1362 date on the KRS may be significant. Perhaps, in anticipation of the conflict, or as a result of it, some monks fled Gotland, and in some unusual turn of events, ended up sailing to Vinland. Monks from Gotland may have been established in Vinland prior to that time, which would explain why it was a destination where their brothers might seek refuge. Another possibility is that monks from Gotland, who were working elsewhere in Scandinavia as stone masons, had no reason to return after the Danish conquest, and so opted to try some new adventure in Vinland.

The fourteenth century in Northern Europe was a remarkably violent period within the Roman Catholic Church, where those seen as heretics were tortured to death and some monastic organizations were completely suppressed. It could be that the Goths who carved the Kensington inscription fled to Vinland because they were being persecuted as heretics. According to Heer, the Church began persecuting the monastic spiritual orders in the mid-13th century and continued to do so for about 150 years, which drove them underground or forced them to flee to other countries and overseas (Heer 1961: 238). Heer wrote that Pope John XXII (1316–34) excommunicated the Spiritual Franciscans, the Waldensians, Cathars and Beguines. The next Pope, Benedict XII (1334–52) continued relentless persecution and was known as the "scourge of heretics." He was followed by Clement VI who focused on the arts and charity. However, his successor, Pope Innocent VI (1352–62) had been an inquisitor and was a remorseless persecutor of Spiritual Franciscans (Heer 1961: 280). Innocent VI was Pope during the decade previous to the date on the KRS, and his renewal of persecutions to stamp out the spiritual thinkers in the Church may have been what drove the Goths to Vinland. Many of the spiritual writers in the Church were German and it is very possible that some were associated with the Goths on Gotland.

Aside from theological reasons, allegations of heresy were one way to eliminate enemies and seize their property. One famous instance occurred in 1305, when the Templars, an order of knights who had fought the Church's battles in the Crusades, eventually grew to be a very wealthy and powerful organization. They were condemned by the Pope for dubious reasons beyond the scope of this book, causing some to flee into hiding. The Templars' assets included a fleet of 18 ships, all of which put out to sea and escaped seizure, but were never heard of again. Much has been written about how the Templars continued their work as an underground organization engaged in virtuous adventures. There is no evidence to identify the Goths who carved the KRS as later generation Templars, but the story of the Templars is an example of one of many bloody conflicts within the Church in the 14th century, when monks fled for their lives and went into hiding.

The Teutonic Knights were a militant order that became dominant in the Prussian region of Germany. In the 14th century, with the crusades to the Holy Land abandoned, they focused their efforts in the Baltic, where Gotland is located, and campaigned to convert the eastern Baltic region to Christianity by armed force. The Cross and the sword went side by side when monastic missionaries undertook to make new converts during the medieval period (Lekai 1953: 50). Those activities may have crossed paths or purposes with some monks on Gotland, who chose flight to some distant place like Vinland to avoid being required to become Teutonic warriors. Or, perhaps the Goths were Teutonic Knights who found themselves accused of crime, justly or not, and so fled.

The prolonged conflict known to history as the Hundred Years War occupied much of the 14th century. In Sweden, conflict was also internal. Fryxell described the Folkungar dynasty that ended in 1374, as follows:

Thus ended the Folkungar dynasty in Sweden, which for 120 years had filled the country with war and bloodshed; for not a King of this race is to be found who did not commit violence on, and act treacherously by his nearest relations, father, brother, and children. They were the cause of their own ruin by their persecutions of each other, to the degree that no noble branch remained of a family once so numerous (Fryxell 1844: 265).

Considering all the hazards of that period, within the Church and out, we should not be surprised that a small group of monks opted to leave for some remote corner of the world, to find peace, concentrate on spiritual matters, to live a simple life, or to perhaps search for new places to carry the faith. All of those goals were consistent with the vision of St. Bernard of Clairvaux, who founded the Cistercian Monastic Order. By the 14th century the Cistercians had been established in Scandinavia for several hundred years. An important Cistercian monastery, Gutnalia, was located 17 kilometers south of Visby, on Gotland. Cistercian historian James France notes that because Christianity was weak in Scandinavia, the orders there would fill their ranks with literate and intelligent persons from Germany and England (France 1992: 6). That observation confirms outside language influences. He also notes that Cistercians, in order to be far away from the turmoil of the world, chose island locations, or sites mostly bounded by water; which reminds us that the Kensington inscription was made on an island. He also states that the Scandinavian orders suffered a decline from 1330 to 1360 because of famine, followed by the plague, which also reappeared in 1356. That decline may have forced some to leave the shelter of the monastery, particularly stone masons, who may have had no work. Another way in which the plague was costly to the Cistercians was that the severe decline in population reduced the need and demand for food, resulting in a major loss of funds from the sale of food products which had been their chief source of income (France 1992: 366).

The Goths and the Norrmen named on the KRS may well have had different social status. The Cistercian Monks routinely had lower ranking associates, known as Conversi, who did much of the physical work. Perhaps the Goths were the monks and the Norrmen were Conversi. Another possibility is that the monks (presumably the Goths) employed the Norrmen as servants both for protection and to provide transportation. Perhaps the Norrmen were experienced sailors residing at a seaport near where the monks were working as stone masons, and because of a sudden outbreak of the Black Death, the monks wished to leave or escape by sea and hired the Norrmen sailors and their ship. They may have known of other monks who had previously relocated in Vinland, so they decided that joining them was their safest course.

In the 14th century, while travel was uncommon and very hazardous, it was less dangerous for those in the Church because the Church had a wide network of abbeys and convents where safe refuge and hospitality for churchmen was available. Monks and clergy were seen to be under God's special care which inhibited many bandits who otherwise attacked vulnerable travelers. Church travel also included the pilgrimage. Geoffrey Chaucer (born about 1340 and thus a contemporary of the author of the Kensington inscription), mentioned Gotland (spelling it Gootland) in the "Prologue" of his *Canterbury Tales*. Chaucer's *Canterbury Tales* describe a mixed group of individuals who set out on a journey that was a religious pilgrimage. Chaucer assumed that his readers would feel that making a religious pilgrimage was a normal event. It may well be that the creators of the KRS saw themselves on a pilgrimage for some purpose.

Nicholas of Lynn, a Franciscan friar, is thought by some to have been an acquaintance of Chaucer who between 1330 and 1360 undertook expeditions and geographical surveys commissioned by King Edward III of England. His work culminated in a 1360 manuscript and map which included North America, called *Inventio Fortunatae* (Thompson 1996: v). Unfortunately that work has been lost and so cannot be evaluated. If there is truth to the story of Nicholas of Lynn and his work, it would be another example of individuals from the monastic world of the Church exploring North America only a few years prior to the KRS.

Gotland did not escape the Black Death. One of the more ruthless or primitive reactions to the disease occurred on Gotland, where a group of nine people were accused of introducing the Black Death to the community, and as punishment were burned at the stake (Scott 1977: 57). That harsh judgment was a clear warning to any thoughtful person that the Black Death was not only a disease that threatened one's life, but also carried the risk that someone could be accused of complicity when others were stricken, and be put to death on that account. The lesson to be learned was that if a new outbreak of the Black Death did subsequently occur on Gotland, people associated with the incident might fear that they would be accused of causing it. Thus an outbreak could have prompted a group of monks to leave the island for a location beyond the reach of the Island's authorities. In such a case, while the individuals would have had no intent to spread disease, it certainly was possible that they might carry fleas that were infected with the plague, and so were capable of setting off an outbreak of the Black Death on Gotland, or anywhere else.

Skeptics of the KRS seem to assume that carving the inscription was a simple task, like writing a postcard to send home while on vacation. To the contrary, the fact is that it required a high degree of skill. The KRS inscription was carved in a very hard stone— graywacke. Craftsmen with the ability to work in stone are uncommon today and history demonstrates that the ability to carve inscriptions in stone has never been a common skill. If one reviews a long list of explorers, including Columbus, Cabot, Verrazano, Cartier, Frobisher, Hudson, Drake, Raleigh, Ponce de Leon, Cortez, De Soto, Coronado, Amerigo Vespucci, Marquette, and La Salle—none left an inscription carved in stone. The rarity of explorers' inscriptions carved in stone simply reinforces the point that to identify who carved the KRS, one must look for skilled stone workers. Gotland was the prime source of craftsmen skilled in stone masonry in the 14th century and was the home of the Goths.

In recent centuries the Roman Catholic Church and some Protestant denominations have viewed Freemasonry with hostility. However, it is very likely that much of the Masonic ritual evolved from rituals in monastic orders of the medieval Church, and that medieval secular craft guilds of stone workers also adopted rituals that were similar to monastic rituals. This is not surprising because the Roman Catholic Church was a major employer of stone craftsmen, who no doubt were influenced by the Church. The fraternal organization known to the modern world as Freemasonry, traces its beginning to Scotland in 1717, which means that it began some 355 years after the KRS. Nevertheless Freemasonry did not emerge from a vacuum. Freemasonry's most noted historian, Dr. Albert G. Mackey, the principal author of *The History of Freemasonry*, published in 1898, states that the traveling freemasons, builders, or operative masons of the Middle Ages, were the real predecessors of the freemasons of the 18th century (Mackey 1898: 367). By looking to modern Freemasonry we get some insight into the medieval craft ceremonial practices. This is important because the structure and rites of the Midewiwin Society of the Ojibway Indians are similar to those of Freemasonry, which suggests that they have something in common. That subject will be considered in the chapter on the Ojibway Indians, but is mentioned here because it also reinforces the fact that the ability to work in stone is one key to the identity of the creators of the KRS.

Another reason why 14th century stone masons operated like a monastic order was because many were free of feudal tenure. This put them outside of the usual restraints that limited the freedom of most people during the feudal period. The reason was that the need for skilled stone masons was irregular. When a project was completed, the stone masons had to move on, so travel was part of their life. Those free from feudal tenure were called free masons, which most likely is the source of the modern term, Freemasonry.

Because they were not under the control of a feudal lord, they would have been free to become explorers if they chose, which was an opportunity not available to most of the population. They also may have been involuntary explorers if their real purpose in fleeing Europe was simply to escape.

For several hundred years before the 14th century, Norway had based its sea trade and military defense on a system whereby each one of nearly 300 seaports or districts was required to build and man one ship—which was the classic long ship, partly powered by oars. In the 13th century a new style of ship, known as the *kogge*, was developed, powered only by sails, which was superior for both trade and combat. Because their ships had become obsolete, the Norwegians abandoned their system in about 1350 (Gjerset 1915: 12). Presumably many of the old ships were seaworthy and thus became available for other uses. The combined factors of general economic depression, a society decimated by the Black Death, and obsolete ships with unemployed crews means that conditions were unusually favorable for a group of monks to arrange a voyage to Vinland.

In the mid–fourteenth century in Northern Europe, very few persons were able to read or write in any language. The very few books which existed were normally made by copying by hand onto thin layers of sheepskin. The author of the KRS inscription was a literate person, a rarity for his time. Someone from Northern Europe in the 14th century who was literate was almost certainly a leader in, or closely connected to, the Church. One explanation for the mixed use of language in the KRS inscription is that its author had picked up his language knowledge from various sources, and was not well educated. Part of his knowledge may have come from studying runic figures in old carved inscriptions, and part may have come from other sources. The KRS inscription may have been a team effort where several men worked out what seemed to them to be the correct way to write the message, and then the inscription was carved by an illiterate stone worker who simply copied the text the others had composed.

Another criticism of the Kensington inscription is that it contained no personal names. However, in a monastic order an individual's name and family connection become less important. The members are brothers. Scandinavians until recently usually did not have family surnames. Instead their custom was to add the word son or daughter to the father's first name to form a last name with the result that family names were not preserved from generation to generation, while place or farm names were carried on indefinitely. Also, there were too many explorers to begin listing all of them. If the inscription was fake, probably the forger would have also made up one or more names.

The date, 1362, in the Kensington inscription is late medieval. It predates the voyage of Columbus in 1492 by only 130 years. Scholars mark the close of the Viking Age with the death of the Norwegian King, Harold Hardrada, in the battle at Stamford Bridge, in the North of England, in 1066. The Viking Age ended long before the date on the KRS, so any notion that the inscription was carved by Vikings is mistaken.

The Black Death

I T IS DIFFICULT FOR MODERN MAN TO GRASP THE enormity of the Black Death in Europe in 1346–50, when an estimated 25 million Europeans died from a disease that was a mystery, without known cause, which seemed to appear suddenly from nowhere in a completely arbitrary fashion, and which after the early terrible years, continued to flare up for over a century. The Church, which had long dominated the European medieval world, taught that disease was God's judgment and punishment. That belief left medieval Europeans to ponder why God had sent the Black Death.

The term, "Black Death," was not used in Europe at the time of the heaviest outbreak, but was coined centuries later, the term's first usage being noted in Sweden in 1555 and in England after 1665 (Ziegler 1971: 17). Because in both the pneumonic and the septicemic forms, the victims coughed up blood as they died, a more apt name would have been the "red death." In the primary septicemic form the victims bleed from the nose and also discharge bloody urine. In the pneumonic end form of either type the victims may bleed profusely from the mouth from internal hemmorhaging. By 1362, the date on the KRS, every European adult must have thought himself lucky to have survived the disease, and yet each also feared that he might well be its next victim. Those fears must have manifested themselves in many unusual ways. Whatever way a man of 1362 may have dealt with the issue, we may be sure that it was much on his mind. From the perspective of an adult in 1362, the plague in Northern Europe remained an essentially contemporaneous event. When the author of the KRS inscription prepared a text for an inscription telling of the sudden deaths, and gross hemmorhaging, of ten of his companions, it never occurred to him that a reader many years in the future would not understand that he was describing the effects of the disease that by then had been devastating his world for about 15 years.

In the 14th century no one had any concept of the existence of bacteria, much less that it caused disease. Today, the Black Death of the 14th century is understood to have been a bacterial infection. It was the bubonic plague, either alone or possibly in combination with another virulent disease as Graham Twigg writes. Would it have been possible for the bubonic plague to have been carried over the Atlantic and then into the heart of North America where it flared up with deadly results? Based on the modern understanding of the bubonic plague the answer is clearly, yes.

Medical research in the 20th century finally led to the discovery that the bubonic plague was spread by fleas. The bacillus, *Yersinia pestis*, which causes the bubonic plague, was first identified in 1894. It required about another forty years for scientists to clearly understand how the disease spread to man. At first, most believed that rats carried the disease to man, because rats were obviously involved in its spread. But it was finally discovered that the infected flea was responsible. The bubonic plague is primarily a disease of wild rodents, and has also been found in many other animals including wild rabbits and coyotes (Burnet and White 1972: 225). The reason why it took many years before the flea was identified as the primary carrier was because many experiments with fleas were inconclusive, since they were done with non-infected fleas. It was finally discovered that before the flea can spread the disease, it first develops the disease itself by feeding on an infected host, such as a rodent. As the disease advances in the insect the infected flea's digestive system becomes blocked.

When the host rodent dies the flea drops off the body. Some time later, after locating a new host, the "blocked" flea attempts to eat again, but it is unable to take in additional blood because of its blocked condition. Instead the flea regurgitates infected blood from its system into the tissue of its new host, thus infecting the new host with the bubonic plague (Hirst 1953: 185).

The ability of an infected, or blocked, flea to spread the disease depends then on how long it can survive. The explorers who created the KRS may or may not have been involved in initially bringing the plague from Europe. The transportation of the disease probably involved several steps. Initially, when the plague was carried to Vinland, it probably resulted in an outbreak in the European and Indian communities in that area, that resulted in new fleas becoming infected. Possibly it was the new outbreak of the Black Death in Vinland that prompted the explorers to leave for the west, because they feared that remaining in Vinland increased their risk of being stricken. They did not realize that they carried the plague with them, in the bodies of infected fleas, which were probably hidden in animal hides they used to carry their weapons and tools.

A key factor that determines the longevity of an infected flea is the temperature. Infected fleas die quickly in hot weather, but in cool temperatures they can live for a long time. In his book, *The Conquest of Plague,* Doctor L. Fabian Hirst reports various experiments on the longevity of infected fleas at various places and at various temperatures, with results showing that infected fleas can survive for over a year (Hirst 1953: 330). Hirst concluded: "there seems no reason to doubt the theoretical possibility that infection might be carried in the bodies of live, unfed fleas halfway round the globe, provided the temperature in the ship's hold seldom exceeded 15 degrees Centigrade" (Hirst 1953: 327).

Other researchers have reported experimental results showing that infected fleas have survived for over a year without a rodent host, which means that long surviving fleas can then infect a new generation of rats to carry the disease over to a new season.

Temperatures in Scandinavia, the North Atlantic, the Gulf of St. Lawrence, the Great Lakes area and in central Minnesota would be sufficiently cool to provide an environment in which fleas could survive for a long period of time, long enough to still be alive and hungry for a new feeding when they crept from the hides where they lurked and came in direct contact with men.

Animal hides were frequent hiding places for infected fleas. There have been a number of instances where bubonic plague was introduced after being transported in cargoes of hides from Spain in 1647, from Turkey in 1790 and from Egypt in 1813 (Hirst 1953: 320). There is also risk of infection from wearing clothing and garments worn by bubonic plague patients. An outbreak in Glasgow, Scotland, in 1900, was thought to have originated from rags (Hirst 1953: 320).

There are three forms of the bubonic plague: bubonic, septicemic, and pneumonic. A human bitten by an infected flea will likely develop the bubonic form, which has a mortality rate of 25–60 percent, if untreated.

The septicemic is the bubonic plague as a type of blood poisoning. This is a primary form of the disease where the infection develops in the blood without the usual initial bubonic symptoms. It develops much more quickly than the usual bubonic form, in one to three days, and is almost always fatal. In the pneumonic form, the initial bubonic plague progresses into the pneumonic form, as the victim develops pneumonia. Once a person with the bubonic plague has developed pneumonia he can discharge infectious bacilli directly into the air from his lungs, which can then spread to other humans by inhalation, causing the recipient to then develop a primary pneumonic plague without having any contact with an infected flea, and without first having the bubonic form (Lefrock, Moldavi and Lentneck 1984: 340). Death from the pneumonic form of the plague follows in nearly all cases within three or four days unless the victim is treated with antibiotics (Lefrock, Moldavi and Lentneck 1984: 341). The incubation of the plague resulting from a bite by an infected flea is one to

12 days, while for primary pneumonic plague only two or three days is required. Sometimes the early stages of the pneumonic form do not present obvious symptoms, and in those instances a victim may not have appeared to be ill until the disease reached its climax, and so it could appear as though the victim had been suddenly stricken down. It seems clear that in 14th century Europe, during the periods when the plague was striking down thousands of victims in mass waves of death, that it was the pneumonic form which was being quickly spread from person to person, by inhalation of the bacteria from discharges from infected persons, or by direct contact with victims or their bodies, or clothing.

It is not difficult to understand how events may have unfolded. Most likely one or more explorer was bitten by plague–infected fleas which had been carried by them in their baggage, and so one or more of them developed bubonic plague. Then the disease progressed into the pneumonic form. The other explorers presumably assisted their stricken comrade and in the process became infected from the lung discharges of the pneumonia victims, and so those giving aid and comfort developed the primary pneumonic form of the disease. Probably these men were strong persons who likely could handle the early stages of their pneumonic plague without obvious symptoms, but did not feel well enough to go fishing, and so stayed behind. During the absence of the fishermen the pneumonia reached its climax in those who had contracted it, and they died, coughing up blood—thus creating the scene described in the inscription. When the author of the KRS inscription wrote that the dead men were "red with blood" he was telling what had happened, as best as he was able, by precisely describing what he had observed, without interpretation, assumptions or judgments.

It should also be pointed out that the inscription does not say that all of those who had not gone fishing, died. It only says that when those who had gone fishing returned, they found ten men dead. That leaves open the possibility that some who had remained behind did not die. A person who has once had the bubonic plague and survived, acquires immunity. Because some or all of the explorers had lived for many years in an environment heavy with the bubonic plague, it would be very likely that some of them would have been plague survivors who were protected by such immunity.

Few fishing trips have ever been memorialized by an inscription carved in stone, so the fact that fishing was mentioned in the Kensington inscription has been the basis for ridicule of the inscription by some critics. However, we must appreciate that it was a common 14th century belief that disease was a punishment or judgment by God upon man. Thus the fact that the author of the Kensington inscription included the detail about being away fishing when his comrades died, could be understood as an affirmation of innocence. It probably was very important to the 14th century monk who wrote the inscription to make it clear that the explorers were doing honest work, and were free from sin. While we should assume that the survivors accepted the deaths of their comrades as the will of God, it is understandable that they still wished to affirm their innocence.

Another reason to understand the KRS inscription as a report of the Black Death is the portion translated as: "AVM save us from illi, illu, or illy." Medieval Christians prayed to be saved from the Black Death with those words. When researching the KRS, Winchell interviewed the Rev. O. A. Norman, who he reports as saying that in an old Norsk song of the 14th century the refrain was a repetition of the line, "AVM, save us from the evil," which was a plea in common use in connection with the burials of those who died of the Black Death. Winchell then wrote: "Note. Was the article 'the' which must have been used in a definite sense (the evil, i.e. the black plague) also on the rune stone? It would indicate, if so used, a literal transcription of a line then in common use at the burials of the black plague victims. It is my impression that it has been sometimes translated 'the evil.'" Winchell's report of that interview was included by Professor Blegen in Appendix 8 of his book on the KRS (Blegen 1968: 150). Blegen also included another reference to a song reported by Professor Ole Eriksson Hagen, a linguist with a Ph.D from the University of Leipzig. Hagen had written that the occurrence of similar language in the old ballad established its 14th century usage. The language from the ballad that Hagen mentioned was quoted and translated by Blegen as follows:

Hjelpe os Gud a Maria moy.
(Help us, God and Virgin Mary,)
A frels os alle av illi!
(And save us all from evil!) (Blegen 1968: 107).

I contend that the word "illy" used in the inscription was intended to describe what we today call an illness. In the context of Scandinavia in the 14th century, the word "illy" often meant the bubonic plague, an illness. It was not used for murder victims or for those lost in battle. The usage in the song reported by Rev. Norman was an example of "illy" used specifically to describe the Black Death. Modern dictionaries supply many definitions of the word evil, one of which is illness. Today we usually define evil as violating or acting inconsistent with moral law, and the word illness means a state of bad health which few would think to call an evil. However, 14th century man had no understanding of disease and often saw illness as an integral part of, or the result of, evil.

Another reason why the KRS inscription should be read as a report of death from disease and not from an assault is that the account of men returning from fishing does not suggest a hostile environment. Another reason is that splitting a graywacke boulder, hammering one side to a smooth finish, and then carving the runes, took considerable time, and made loud noise that would have given away their location if they had any concern about attack. If such a battle had occurred any inscription would have given us more details, rather than telling of fishing.

The proposition that the Black Death of 14th century Europe reached North and South America has substantial scientific support. Because the plague is a disease of wild rodents and not of man, the disease has received considerable attention in veterinary medicine. *Black's Veterinary Dictionary* states that "nearly 5000 human cases were reported between 1960–69 in South America" (West 1992: 84). "The Morbidity and Mortality Weekly Report," published by the Center for Disease Control in Atlanta, Georgia, periodically publishes reported cases of the plague in the United States.

Studies of the plague show that it is primarily a disease of wild rodents and not of man, and may exist in an area without human cases due to lack of exposure to rodent and flea sources. In an article on the Plague published in 1989, Dennis W. Macy, D.V.M. reported that "230 species of wild rodents have been naturally infected with the plague organism (sylvatic plague) and over 1500 species of fleas have been shown to transmit *Y. pestis.*" He wrote that plague is endemic in foci in the semiarid regions of 15 western states from Mexico to the Canadian border but that 90 percent of the human cases have been reported in New Mexico, Arizona, and California (Macy 1989: 1088).

Two doctors, Larry D. Crook and Bruce Tempest, reviewed 27 cases of human plague seen at a medical center at Gallup, New Mexico, between 1965 and 1989. Of these, 19 had bubonic plague with three deaths, eight had septicemic plague also with three deaths, and of the 27 cases, four had developed the pneumonic form. Plague is treatable with antibiotics, but sometimes the disease is not correctly diagnosed in time for proper treatment. The New Mexico doctors concluded, "The six deaths in our series were related to the failure to consider the correct diagnosis and give appropriate antibiotics initially. If the death rate from plague is to be lowered, clinicians must maintain a very high index of suspicion and administer antibiotics effective against plague at the earliest opportunity to patients whose presentation suggests the possibility of plague" (Crook and Tempest 1992: 1256).

It has been found that rodents spend their lives within a small territory, and that it is only when man becomes involved in the disease cycle that the plague is carried for long distances. Once introduced into an area, the plague often persists indefinitely, not necessarily as a major threat to the human populations, but as a residual disease that continues in the local rodent population. The fact is that *Yersinia pestis,* the bacteria that causes the plague, is found today in wild rodents over wide areas of North and South America. Because history was silent on any introduction of the plague from Europe, experts have explained the presence of *Yersinia pestis* in the Americas by pointing out the possibility that it was introduced from Asia in 1874. It certainly is possible that such an introduction occurred, however it seems unlikely that such a recent introduction could have spread *Yersinia pestis* over such a large area into so many different rodent populations. However, if one also accepts the proposition that a major introduction of the plague also occurred in the 14th century, then its wide distribution among many rodent populations can be understood as the natural residual consequence of that introduction, and subsequent transportation over the Americas.

The Black Death struck Europe in 1346, and had reached Scandinavia by 1349. Because of its enormity it is termed a pandemic rather than merely an epidemic. It is estimated to have caused 25 million deaths, killing from 25 to 50 per cent of the population and in some communities all died. Strangely enough, the Black Death itself did not reach Iceland until 1402, some 53 years after it first arrived in Norway, and 40 years after the date of the KRS inscription. There seems to be no account of how the plague entered Iceland in 1402, but it was extremely severe, killing as many as two-thirds of the population in two years (Headley 1874: 265 and Gjerset 1924: 257). Why it was that the Black Death reached Iceland so many years after it hit Northern Europe is a mystery. One possibility is that the Black Death reached Iceland in 1402 from North America, arriving there in furs being smuggled into the European fur trade. Icelandic records report that 1347 a ship left Greenland for Markland (a Labrador site) and was driven by storms and landed in Iceland, with seventeen men on board (Gjerset 1924: 245). That indicates that North American place names were known in Iceland in the 14th century. Norwegian trade regulations controlling Iceland were very strict and so if any Icelandic sailors were involved in the fur trade between America and Europe they would have kept it a close secret. Prior to the time of the Black Death, Norwegian sea trade was flourishing. Gjerset reports its extent as follows: "Traffic was maintained with Flanders, northern Germany, southern Sweden, the island of Gothland and other places, but especially with England, where Lynn was a Norwegian trade center" (Gjerset 1924: 228). The Norwegian trade could have easily been the way that information about Iceland and Vinland was passed along to smugglers.

The historical impact of the introduction of the Black Death into the New World in the 14th century is considered in the final chapter of this book: The Open Land.

The Language of
the Rune Stone

T HE CRITICS WHO HAVE CALLED THE KRS A HOAX
have mainly based their objection on linguistic grounds,
claiming that the inscription contains runic usages that
were not attributable to the 14th century, and that the Arabic
numbering system was not used at that time. To meet such
claims, the proponents of the authenticity of the inscription have
searched the historical record looking for 14th century examples
of the questioned usages. The most recent and thorough work on
the linguistic issues has been done by a private scholar from Denmark, Richard Nielsen, who has built on the research done by
Hjalmar Holand and Robert A. Hall. Nielsen's articles have appeared in volumes 15, 16 and 17 of ESOP, a publication of occasional papers by the Epigraphic Society. Nielsen's work cites
many specific examples of the disputed KRS runes in 14th century usages, particularly on Gotland.

It now is clear that the critics of the KRS rested their claims of
a hoax on their own lack of knowledge. A fair assessment of Nielsen's work leads to the conclusion that no one, neither Olof
Ohman nor the top linguistic scholars in Scandinavia, could have
written the KRS inscription in the late 19th century based on
what was known about runes at that time.

Now that the message in the inscription can be correctly understood, only one change in the commonly accepted translation
of the Kensington inscription is indicated. That change is the last

word in the prayer. As I have explained, it should read: save us from illness, rather than: save us from evil. Nielsen shows both meanings for the word in his work (Nielsen 1988: 138, 149, 161). When we understand that the ten men who died had not been killed, but had died from illness, the otherwise ambiguous understanding of that word is resolved.

The study of ancient language and writing practice, like all historical study, relies on assumptions and perspective. Aside from their lack of knowledge of 14th century runic usage, I believe that the linguistic critics of the KRS inscription were mistaken because they assumed that in order for it to be authentic, it should reflect the work of a well educated individual who followed the standards of grammar and runic usages found in texts of church law or classic poems. However, the KRS inscription was not created by a scholar.

In 1362 when the inscription was made, many variations in language, spelling of words, and manner of usage, were the rule, not the exception. Considering the general lack of literacy in medieval Scandinavia, the true circumstances probably were that the explorers, including the stone masons who carved the inscription, were, at best, only semi-literate. While the party included expert stone carvers who carved the inscription, they most likely were craftsmen who worked by following drawings prepared by others. They were not writers or editors. Literacy was rare in the fourteenth century and there would have been little opportunity or need for a stone carver to have been able to read or write in order to follow drawings prepared by others. We can appreciate the situation better if we consider how the KRS inscription most likely was created. It was not a casual note, like a tourist might write on a postcard. The inscription supplies a great deal of information in few words and must have been drafted after considerable thought. Because the message was to be carved in stone it was appreciated that it must be concise. Several members of the group probably considered and discussed the text. They did very well because in a few words the text identifies the explorers—tells where they came from—tells their purpose—reports their activities—describes their misfortune—describes three of their relevant locations—utters a prayer for their safety—and reports their care of their ships. Once they had agreed on the text, they had to prepare drawings of the runes to be carved to tell the message. Drawing the runes may well have involved considerable discussion. Some may have been familiar with runes based on their experience in carving, but lacked sufficient knowledge of grammar and usages to correctly write the text. Some may have recalled old runic inscriptions which contained usages that by then were archaic. Perhaps there were disagreements, settled by compromise. Therefore it is not surprising that their finished product differs from what a learned scholar of the time might have written.

Literacy was rare in the fourteenth century. It was mostly limited to the Church, and even then, many priests worked only from rote memory and could not read. No doubt literacy was even more rare among the craft trades. While it is difficult today to understand how rare literacy was in the 14th century, we must also appreciate the fact that the written languages of those who were literate were evolving. For example, Shakespeare lived and wrote approximately two centuries after 1362; and yet in the six known examples of his signature, he spelled his name differently in each instance. In the 14th century the Swedish and Gotlandic languages were different enough, so that centuries later those differences continued to be sufficient to warrant publication of a Swedish-Gotlandic dictionary. Probably the explorers came from different countries and backgrounds. If, as I believe, the author, or authors, were Roman Catholic monks, probably of the Cistercian Order, it may well be that some of them had lived and worked previously in England, Denmark, Norway and Sweden or in other places around the Baltic Sea. They may have had teachers or colleagues who came from elsewhere in Europe. Therefore, it is impossible for any linguist today to evaluate the language or runic usage done by one or more of those monks, as found in the

KRS inscription, and then on the basis of irregularities or English or German influence, to correctly judge it a hoax.

Historian Frederick Jackson Turner was wise when he commented on the KRS inscription in 1910, and noted his skepticism of the linguistic critics by observing that rules are formulated from inscriptions, as well as inscriptions tested by rules (Blegen 1968: 63).

To sum up the linguistic issue it seems that we are left with the fact, that while obscure or uncommon, all of the runic characters, or vocabulary found in the KRS can be attributed to mid-14th century usage on Gotland. Further, because many aspects were unusual enough to stump many scholars who have considered the inscription in the past, it establishes that no modern forger could have known enough to have adopted those obscure usages. The endless linguistic debate about the KRS has resembled the trial of a legal case where each side hires an expert witness, who then contradicts the other. Often in such cases the jury will rely mainly on other evidence for their verdict. We now understand the true message of the KRS inscription and the circumstances of the stone's creation and burial. With that new outlook, the linguistic debate will probably fade away.

✦ Part II ✦

The Dakota Contact

The Dakota Homeland

WHEN THE EUROPEAN EXPLORERS WHO CARVED
the KRS reached the western end of Lake Superior,
they had entered the homeland of the Dakota Indians. While the Dakotas lived in small groups throughout the
area, the most important Dakota Indian population concentra-
tion was in the region of Lake Mille Lacs in what is now Minnesota (Brower and Bushnell 1900: 95; and Blegen 1963: 20).
Knife Lake, on Knife River, was approximately 18 miles southeast
of Lake Mille Lacs, when traveling via Knife River for most of
the distance. Edward D. Neill, one of the founders of the Minnesota Historical Society, in his *History of Minnesota from the
Earliest French Explorations to the Present Time*, wrote:

> Tradition says that it [Spirit Lake] was a day's walk from
> Isantamde or Knife Lake . . . and the Spirit Lake on which
> they dwelt was, without doubt, Mille Lac of modern charts
> (Neill 1882: 52).

Neill's 1882 account reporting the Dakota tradition that Knife
Lake was a day's walk from Mille Lacs immediately brings to
mind the KRS inscription which describes the location where the
ten men were found dead, to have been one day's journey north of
the island where the rune stone was carved. Knife Lake contains
a number of islands, including one fairly large island near where
Knife River enters the lake. That island probably is the site where

the KRS was carved and erected. Both the lake and stream have the same name: "Knife."

To find evidence of Dakota Indian-European contact in the 14th century, probably the best place to start is to consider what Dakota Indians have said about it. Anthropologists have assumed that these Dakota reports were myths or legends. However, if one takes them as essentially factual accounts as seen or understood from the Dakota perspective, it seems clear that they have been telling of their 14th century encounter with Europeans for many years.

It is my hypothesis that the explorers who carved the KRS may have had a number of goals. Assuming that they were led by Christian monks, one would certainly have been to teach the Christian faith to the Indians whenever the opportunity presented itself. Assuming that the circumstances of illness and death of many members of their party delayed the explorers and prolonged their stay with the Dakotas from winter until the next spring, giving them ample time to teach their hosts, it would be likely that whatever residual memory of that contact has survived in Indian history or tradition, would reflect Christian teachings.

One of the first published observations describing Dakota Indian beliefs indicating Christian influence was by William H. Keating in his account of an expedition in 1823 to the source of St. Peter's River (now known as the Minnesota River). Keating wrote that while the Dakota had but little contact with missionaries, "still, in some of their credences, as related to us, it was impossible not to discover a few of the doctrines of Christianity, which had probably crept in unnoticed by them" (Keating 1825: 288). There is no record of missionary contact with the Dakota Indians in the area visited by Keating prior to 1823 which would account for the Christian ideas that he noted.

Garrick Mallery, one of the main contributors to the Smithsonian Institution's ethnology studies in the late 19th century, interpreted Dakota Indian pictographic history, or winter counts. In respect to several early examples, he wrote:

These pages are only interesting from the mythology and tradition referred to and suggested by them, and which must be garnered from the chaff of uncomprehended missionary teaching (Mallery 1893: 288).

I believe that Mallery was correct in identifying missionary teaching as the source, however I believe that the teaching took place in the 14th century, not after Columbus' voyages.

The name, Dakota, is a general name that I will use to include many related Indian groups, who use various names; and who live in Minnesota and the Northern Plains. Rather than attempting to trace each subdivision of the Dakota, I have used the name, Dakota, to include them all. While Dakota Indian history includes a number of aspects that reflect influence traceable to contact with the explorers who carved the KRS, it is obvious that only a relatively few Dakota Indians could have had that firsthand contact, and only a small number would remember and pass down that history, and still fewer remained in direct possession of the KRS and the Sacred Pipe. Over the centuries, the ideas that evolved from that 14th century European contact spread to a wider circle of Dakotas, and so by the 20th century, it is unlikely that one could tell how closely associated one group of Dakotas or another was to the original contact. It is also interesting to realize that many Dakota Indians were never well informed about what is called the Dakota Spiritual Tradition because it was passed down within a relatively small leadership group. The reason why Black Elk wanted scholars to record the Dakota's history and tradition as he knew it was because he appreciated the fact that it was not well known by most Dakotas and he feared that it might otherwise be lost to history (Brown 1953: xiv).

As one would expect, the 14th century Dakota grasp of the message brought by the monks was limited. The Dakota Spiritual Tradition evolved in that context. Their mistaken interpretation of what they observed, their lack of understanding of important aspects of the monks' teaching, the passage of many centuries, and the limitations resulting from the lack of a written language, all served to confuse and change much of the Christian message. Nevertheless Dakota Tradition is recalled as a sacred story, and one which Dakota Indians, such as Black Elk, found to be in harmony with Christian belief, to the extent that while Black Elk was a major teacher of the Dakota Spiritual Tradition, at the same time he was a catechist, working as an assistant or lay priest, in the Roman Catholic Church in the Pine Ridge area in South Dakota. In that role he worked to expand the role of the Catholic Church in its ministry to the Dakota (Lakota) people (Steltenkamp 1993: 107). Black Elk reconciled and accepted the Christianity of the Roman Catholic Church and the Dakota Tradition (Holler 1995: 213). His dual role has confused some observers, yet, once we understand that the Dakota Indian Spiritual Tradition originated and evolved from the teachings of European Christian monks in the 14th century, we can understand how Black Elk could be equally comfortable, both as interpreter and teacher of the Dakota Spiritual Tradition and as a catechist in the Roman Catholic Church.

Black Elk's accounts as told to Neihardt and Brown are the most detailed accounts of the many Dakota Rites that I believe originated from their 14th century European contact. Most prominent are the accounts of the White Buffalo Woman and her gift of the Dakota's Sacred Pipe. The Sacred Pipe, like the KRS, is an actual object, not a myth or legend. It was not carved by a mystic spirit, but more probably by one of the more skilled 14th century Europeans. It was presented as a gift to the Dakotas from the Virgin Mary.

In addition to Dakota Tradition, there is significant archaeological evidence of the contact. The archaeological record of the Dakota Indians in the Mille Lacs region, and nearby areas indicates that a definite change occurred in their way of life in the mid-14th century. Professor Guy E. Gibbon in his study, "The Prehistory of the Sioux, 9500 B.C.–A.D. 1650," postulated a model where beginning in the mid-14th century a more advanced social order became established, based on greater economic cooperation. The change was evidenced by larger, more permanent structures. Gibbon reviewed several reasons suggested by others for this social advancement but declined to adopt any as his own. My explanation for the sudden change is that the Europeans, in addition to religious instruction, also taught the Dakota many new craft skills, gave them metal tools and taught them better ways to provide food and shelter for themselves. That new learning enabled the Dakotas to advance into what has been named the Psinomani complex. The Dakota accounts, which are reviewed in the following chapters, say the same.

In the future it may well be that the 14th century contact can be proven from certain archaeological finds in the Mille Lacs area that originated from the explorers during that century and which have not been correctly interpreted; or it may be that greater attention to the region by archaeologists will uncover objects proving the contact.

Susan Windgrow's Story

ASANTEE DAKOTA INDIAN ACCOUNT TELLS, IN CON-
siderable detail, of a friendly visit to the Dakota Indians
by a group of 38 white men many centuries ago. The
story was told by one of the tribal elders, Mrs. Susan Windgrow,
in 1935, when she was about 90 years old. She did not speak English, only Dakota, so she spoke through an interpreter, her
"grandson," Irving Campbell. Windgrow said she had learned
the story years ago, from the "old people." Both Susan Windgrow and Irving Campbell resided at the Prairie Island Reservation on the Mississippi River, near Red Wing, Minnesota. Her
story was recorded by anthropologist Ruth Landes in her book,
The Mystic Lake Sioux: Sociology of the Mdewakantonwan Santee
(1968).

Susan Windgrow said that long ago early in spring her people
saw a ship which had three sails, and which was also powered by
oarsmen. Both ends of the ship and its mastheads were deco-
rated with carved snakes and there were ten shields on each side
of the craft. The visitors wore armor and were armed with spears,
knives and axes on poles. The visitors gave them gifts of knives
and axes and many tools, and had taught them how to use them.
She also told Landes that the visitors were "jolly," but had no
"firewater;" and that they had remained with the Dakota all
summer and over the next winter. Windgrow told Landes that
the visitors did not "marry" Indians, presumably a euphemism to

Susan Windgrow (Makawastewin) with Frances Densmore, at Prairie Island, near Red Wing, Minnesota, 1930.
Susan Windgrow told Ruth Landes the old peoples' story of white visitors.
Photograph courtesy of Minnesota Historical Society.

suggest that the visitors did not have sexual contact with the Dakota women (Landes 1968: 22).

While Susan Windgrow did not mention any specific inland site visited by these explorers, she did say that it was impractical for the visitors to move their big boat overland on skids and so the Dakotas "taught them to use dugout and birch bark canoes, and to portage" (Landes 1968: 23). Portage clearly implies inland travel. The KRS inscription on the side of the stone says that the group of ten men remained with the ships while the 8 Goths and 22 Normen traveled inland. The view of the Dakota storyteller seems to be that the ancestors lived where the ship landed, and so presumably they would have become acquainted with the ten men left to guard the ships. The story that Susan Windgrow repeated to Landes was the Dakota woman's view of the visit by the explorers who carved the KRS. The story does not touch on matters of religious instruction which I believe inspired the Dakota Spiritual Tradition because that religion was a male activity and probably took place only at the inland location in the Mille Lacs region. And, she delves into the subject of the absence of any relationship between the visitors and the Dakota women, which probably would have been of particular interest to the women and probably would not have been mentioned by Dakota men.

Susan Windgrow's story is remarkable in that it says there were 38 white men. The KRS inscription tells of 8 Goths and 22 Northmen, making a group of 30 (ten of whom died suddenly), plus 10 men who were left with their ships, which adds up to a party of 40 men, which is two more than 38. However, the Dakota story mentions only 38 white men, so if the exploring party also included two Indians who had guided the group and who were two of the 10 men left with the ships, then the numbers in the inscription and the Dakota story match.

From the Dakota perspective, that visit must have been seen as amazing, comparable to the way modern man might receive a visitor from outer space. Certainly it was a story to be remembered and repeated, and it is difficult to think that a non-English speaking Dakota woman would be out to create a hoax at the age of 90. Why not believe her?

The Isanti – People
of the Cut Stone

A FTER THE EXPLORERS LEFT THE MILLE LACS—
Knife Lake area, the Dakotas remained in possession of
the KRS, which they saw as a mysterious stone that had
supernatural power. Like the Sacred Pipe, they believed it was a
sacred object that had been entrusted to them to protect and
treasure. Just as the Sacred Pipe was kept in a bundle, they probably were quick also to cover the KRS in order to limit and control
the occasions when its power would be invoked. Probably, when
one achieved high status, he became eligible to join the number of
individuals permitted to view the stone. And presumably there
were times when the stone was unveiled when it became the focal
point for a tribal ceremony. Thus the KRS became a major focus
for those Dakota who had been in contact with the exploring
monks, to the extent that they identified themselves as the Isanti,
meaning the people who possessed "isan," the cut stone.

The runic figures carved in the Kensington Rune Stone were
seen by the Dakota only as cuts in the stone, not as writing. They
had no concept of writing or reading. When the monks had read
the stone's inscription aloud, telling them what it said, the Dakotas probably mistakenly understood that the KRS could speak.
Centuries later, in 1680, Father Louis Hennepin observed that
same response from the Dakotas when, during his stay with them,
he began to write down their vocabulary on paper in order to study
and learn their language. Later, when Hennepin read the words

that he had written on the paper aloud to them, he wrote that they thought that it was the paper talking (Hennepin 1699: 172).

The Dakota belief that the KRS possessed mystic power was most likely the source of their practice of stone worship. They combined that belief with what the monks had taught them about God and the story of creation. That mixture of ideas became the basis from which they developed a native religion, unique to them, that recognized an all powerful spirit God, whom they called Wakan Tanka, who was all present, but particularly present in stones. Edward Neill described Stone worship as follows:

> The hunter, as he passes over the plains, finds a granite boulder: he stops and prays to it, for it is *Wawkawn"*—mysterious or supernatural (Neill 1882: 54).

> When a Dahkotah is troubled in spirit, and desires to be delivered from real or imaginary danger, he will select a stone that is round and portable, and, placing it in a spot free from grass and underbrush, he will streak it with red paint, and, offering to it some feathers, he will pray to it for help (Neill 1882: 60).

Joseph Epes Brown, in *The Spiritual Legacy of the American Indian*, wrote: "abundant recorded materials" established that the Dakota acknowledgment of a Supreme Being, Wakan-Tanka, pre-dated American white settlement and post-Columbian Christian missionaries (Brown 1982: 78). In the same work he also reported the Dakota belief in respect of stones, writing, ". . . even rocks have a life of their own and are believed to be able to talk under certain conditions" (Brown 1982: 71).

The Eleventh Annual Report of the Bureau of American Ethnology, 1889–90, includes a chapter entitled, "A Study of Siouan Cults" by James Owen Dorsey that deals with the Stone God of the Dakotas. It includes a long quote from Rev. Horace C. Hovey, about a particular stone called Red Rock, which was located on the bank of the Mississippi River about midway between present-day St. Paul and Hastings, Minnesota:

It was the custom of the Dakotas to worship boulders when in perplexity and distress. Clearing a spot from grass and brush they would roll a boulder on it, streak it with paint, deck it with feathers and flowers, and then pray to it for needed help or deliverance. Usually when such a stone had served its purpose its sacredness was gone. But the peculiarity of the stone now described is that from generation to generation it was a shrine to which pilgrimages and offerings were made. Its Indian name, "Eyah Shah," simply means the "Red Rock," and is the same term by which they designate catlinite, or the red pipe clay. The rock is not naturally red, being merely a hard specimen of granite, symmetrical in shape, and about 5 feet long by 3 feet thick. The Indians also called it "waukon" (mystery) and speculated as to its origin.... The particular clan that claimed this rude altar was known as the Mendewakantons.... Twice a year the clan would meet more formally, when they would paint the stone with vermilion, or, as some say, with blood, then trim it with flowers and feathers, and dance around it before sunrise with chants and prayers. Their last visit was in 1862, prior to the massacre that occurred in August of that year. Since that date, the stripes were renewed three years ago. I counted the stripes and found them twelve in number, each about 2 inches wide, with intervening spaces from 2 to 6 inches wide.... Eyah Shah lies twelve paces from the main bank of the Mississippi, at a point 6 miles below St. Paul. The north end is adorned by a rude representation of the sun with fifteen rays (Dorsey 1894: 448).

It is interesting to note that according to Hovey, the rock was not red so that red paint was used to symbolize blood. That practice suggests that the Dakota retained an understanding that the KRS inscription made reference to blood.

The word in Dakota that described the Kensington Rune Stone, the cut stone, was "isan" or "issi." Scholars of the language and history of the Dakota Indians have puzzled over the many instances when the word "isan" was used. It was seen to be important because it was a term from which several tribes of Dakota took their name or identity. The word has been written or used in various forms, including: issi, isan, issan, izzaty, issanti, and the term is the base word for the tribal names of Sissitonwans and Sisseton, and Isanti and Sante. Because the word refers to "cut stone" or "cutting" it was assumed by some to refer to the instrument that one would use to cut: that is, "knife." It seems clear that the "knife" interpretation of the term is the source of the names for the Knife Lake and Knife River, which are located near Mille Lacs and which are part of, or along, the most important waterway routes to and from Mille Lacs and the St. Croix River.

When early missionaries reached the Dakota Indians in the 19th century they set about to learn the Dakota language and create a written Dakota version. They approached their work in a scholarly fashion and endeavored to learn the derivation and relationship of the words in the Dakota language. Because the word "isan" was the core word in the name Isanti, some explanation was needed. As one could imagine, the 19th century Dakota had a difficult time trying to explain the word "isan" to the missionaries. Probably only a few of the Dakotas actually knew the true story, and those few were not interested in sharing their sacred secrets with missionaries. The missionaries came to understand that the word involved the concept of cutting and stones, which led them to reason that the term referred to a place where the Indians found sharp stones useful in making knives.

Obviously no one who wrote about the Dakota language and the origin of its terminology in the 19th century ever dreamt that the term "issan" arose because the Dakota who identified themselves with that word once had protected a stone which they had been led to believe possessed mystical power. Nor could scholars imagine that the stone that had initially prompted both the

Dakota's use of the word, and their worship of stones, bore an inscription that had been carved in the 14th century by European explorers. By the time of post-Columbian contact with the Dakota Indians, the KRS was probably either covered and hidden where it had been erected or was kept in a sacred Dakota tribal bundle, the contents of which would have been kept in strict secrecy, even from most tribal members.

Stephen R. Riggs was one of the missionaries who worked with the Dakota Indians who were then living along the Minnesota River (formerly St. Peter's River) in western Minnesota. Riggs edited the first Dakota dictionary, *Grammar and Dictionary of the Dakota Language,* published in 1852 by the Smithsonian Institution. He expressed uncertainty about the words "sisi" and "Isanti," writing "What the meaning of 'sisi' is, we have not been able to ascertain satisfactorily, as we do not find it in any other combination in the language as now used" (Riggs 1852: vii).

In the Dakota to English section of the dictionary "Isanati" is defined as follows:

> The name which is applied to the Dakota of the Mississippi and Minnesota by those living on the Missouri. Why this name has been given to them is still a matter of conjecture; perhaps, because they pitched their tents formerly at Isantamde, or Knife Lake, one of those which go under the denomination of Mille Lacs; or, perhaps, it was given to them because they lived near the Isantanka, or Big-knives, i.e. the Americans (Riggs 1852: 92).

In the English to Dakota section of the dictionary "knife" is defined as "isan" (Riggs 1852: 308).

Riggs refers to the Mille Lacs Dakota as follows: "The Mdewakantonwans Village of the Spirit Lake. Their name is derived from a former residence at Mdewakan (Spirit or Sacred Lake), Mille Lacs ... (Riggs 1852: vii). He also states, "The intercourse between the Mdewakantonwans on the Mississippi and lower Minnesota and the Wahpetonwans, Wahpekutes, and a part of the Sisitonwan family, has been so constant, that but slight variations are discoverable in their manner of speaking" (Riggs 1852: viii). He also described the Dakota reverence toward stones, writing ". . . a Dakota dances in religious homage to the sun and moon, and spreads out his hands in prayer to a painted stone . . ." (Riggs 1852: x).

J. V. Brower and D. I. Bushnell, Jr., in *Memoirs of Explorations in the Basin of the Mississippi*, Vol. III, Mille Lac, included a nomenclature section about Dakota tribal names and wrote of the term "issan" as follows: "In Minnesota a county is named Isanti. Some of the forms of this name are—Isanyatee, Isanati, Sisseton, Santee. 'Isan—knife, ati—dwell.' A portion of the tribe dwelt on Knife River and lake in Kanabec county, near Mille Lac, hence the name" (Brower and Bushnell 1900: 42).

In Vol. IV of that series, entitled *Kathio*, published in 1901, J. V. Brower wrote as follows:

> Mr. Louis Marlow, the Sisseton interpreter, recently stated that the name "Issati" or "Isanti" came from the fact that the Isanti people first came into the possession of iron or steel knives, possibly during Radisson's time, and for that reason were called "knife" people. It would naturally follow that the lake and river of that name, where they resided, became historically known as Knife lake and river, after the name of the inhabitants (Brower 1901: 43–44).

N. H. Winchell, longtime state geologist, and author of the monumental book, *Aborigines of Minnesota* (1911), did not accept Brower's theory, but he did agree with him there were no sharp or slate-like stone deposits in the Lake Mille Lacs and Knife Lake region that would account for the name (Winchell 1911: 340). In respect to Brower's reference to the Radisson gift of knives, Winchell wrote that the name could not have been established in so short a time:

> If, therefore, the designation Issati originated, as supposed by Mr. Brower, from their having first received knives from

the French in 1660, and that hence the river along which they chiefly dwelt became known as Knife River, the period of 19 years between Radisson and Du Luth, was sufficient not only to establish the tribal name Issati, but to transfer it to the chief settlement at Mille Lacs. The improbability of the spread of the name in that manner in that space of time casts a doubt on such supposed origin (Winchell 1911: 340).

Winchell's *Aborigines of Minnesota* and Brower's several books reporting excavations and findings in the Mille Lacs region do not consider the possibility that in some instances what they found was evidence of pre-Columbian contact. They were not looking for medieval European contact, and because they had little knowledge about that period it may well be that they failed to recognized such evidence. It seems to me that a careful study of their work by qualified specialists might correctly identify evidence that relates to the 1362 visit. Specifically I have in mind two large iron spear points which were found by investigators in the Mille Lacs area. The spear points were display at the Mille Lacs Indian museum near the lake for many years. Recently a new museum was built whose exhibits focused on the Ojibway Indians who occupied the area in about 1750. The Dakota-era objects, including the spear points, are no longer on view. Those iron weapons appeared to me to be possibly of medieval origin because they resembled published photographs of European medieval weapons, and they deserve further study. We can assume that the explorers who carved the KRS were well armed with medieval weapons, and that they would have presented some examples of these weapons to the Dakotas, and those gifts could have been the weapons that were on display at Mille Lacs for many years.

Father Hennepin and the Dakota Indians

I N 1680 FATHER LOUIS HENNEPIN WAS THE FIRST Roman Catholic churchman to have had post-Columbian contact with the Dakota Indians. The only known white contacts the Dakotas had prior to Hennepin were Radisson and Groseilliers, about 20 years earlier, and Du Luth (Daniel Greysolon Du Luth), in 1679. Du Luth visited the Dakotas at Mille Lacs in 1679 and returned in 1680. Du Luth and Hennepin traveled together when they returned east in 1680.

Hennepin wrote of his adventures in a book published in Europe in 1683. He was a more thoughtful observer than the fur traders and he was often surprised and amused at Dakota ways. The reason why Hennepin's observations are relevant to the KRS is because he described the unusual ways that the Dakotas treated him; ways that strongly suggest that the Dakotas recalled a connection between their Spiritual Tradition and Europeans. My hypothesis is that the Dakota Spiritual Tradition originated from an extensive 14th century contact with European Catholic monks; and Hennepin's account shows that the Dakotas sought to involve him in their rituals because they saw him as a visitor like those in the past who had taught them their tradition.

When the Dakotas first came upon Hennepin he raised his Calumet, an Indian pipe, as a sign of peace and friendship. Hennepin's religious garb and demeanor probably suggested to them that he might have a relationship to their Spiritual Tradition.

Father Louis Hennepin.
Portrait by unknown artist, circa 1694.
Photograph courtesy of Minnesota Historical Society.

Because the Dakotas were obviously undecided about what to make of Hennepin, it appears that they were probing. Radisson and Groseilliers in 1661 and Du Luth in 1679, seemed only interested in trade and gave no sign of spiritual concern. However, Hennepin was different. He practiced regular religious devotions, and had a demeanor or presence which the Dakotas would have compared to their own medicine or mystical men. Because of language and vocabulary limitations, the Dakotas could not explain their traditions to Hennepin; and he seems to have been unaware that the Dakotas were testing him for his response to their outreach. Hennepin saw the Dakotas as barbarians, so when they sought to draw him into their spiritual circle, Hennepin was only surprised. However, he did record those events for posterity, which gives us an opportunity to consider the reason why the Dakotas attempted to involve Hennepin in their sacred rituals as they did.

First, the Dakotas went to the trouble of transporting him to Mille Lacs. According to Hennepin, he and two companions were captured by a war party of about 120 Dakota Indians, traveling in some 50 canoes, on the Mississippi River probably near the present Iowa and Minnesota border. Once the Dakotas encountered Hennepin, they abandoned their other plans, forcing Hennepin and his two companions to accompany them north, to their home at Mille Lacs. What was so important about Hennepin to cause a large party of Dakota warriors to change their plans and instead transport Hennepin to Mille Lacs, some two hundred miles to the north? The reason, it seems to me, is because their leaders saw Hennepin as a man of special significance, and they entertained the hope that Hennepin's presence represented the return of the mystical white men who had visited and taught their ancestors in the 14th century.

Next came their prodigious weeping. If any aspects of Medieval Christian practices are also aspects of American Indian culture, the more unusual or unique the practice the better the claim is that one introduced the other. One interesting and bizarre practice that was true for both the Cistercian monks and the Dakota Indians was the practice of prodigious weeping. The Cistercians followed a practice of effusive weeping while praying, which France described as "an amazingly unrestrained display of emotion which seems very exaggerated to us . . ." (France 1992: 111). He reported that St. Bernard, founder of the Order, introduced the practice of shedding tears while praying as his way of bringing emotion into Christian spirituality. One description of

St. Bernard of Clairvaux.
St. Bernard was the founder of the Cistercian Order, the white-robed monks, in 1115. This portrait is circa 1152.
From Rev. Ailbe J. Luddy, *The Order of Citeaux* (1932), p. 41.

this Cistercian practice was ". . . the fountain of his tears gushes forth like a deluge flooding the earth." (France 1992: 111). The practice of profuse open weeping recalls a strange and unique exchange that occurred when the Dakota Indians met their first white men. In 1661 two Frenchmen, Pierre Esprit Radisson and Medard Chouart, better known as Des Groseilliers, were travelling along the south shore of Lake Superior until cold weather forced them to land and set up camp for the winter. Several months later both men were near starvation, when to their amazement a party of Dakota Indians approached them bearing large amounts of food. As a part of their welcome, Radisson wrote, "they weeped upon our heads until we were wetted by their tears" (Radisson 1961: 134). Father Hennepin, in 1680, also was wept over by the Dakotas. Hennepin supposed that the weeping reflected the Dakota's disappointment in not being allowed to kill him, but I believe that he, like Radisson, never realized that effusive weeping was a practice that the Dakotas assumed was a regular custom or practice of the white man. This was based upon their observations long ago of profuse open weeping by white men at prayer. Hennepin reports several other occasions when Dakota leaders wept tears over his head where the circumstances clearly show no hostile purpose. One weeping episode, during their trip north on the Mississippi, was described by Hennepin (in the language of the 1699 edition) as follows:

> The next day they left us alone in our Canou, without putting any of their Men a-board to assist us, as they had hitherto done: However, they kept all in the rear of us. After rowing four or five Leagues, another of their Captains came up to us, and made us land. As soon as we got on shoar, he fell to cutting of Grass, which he made into three little Heaps, and bade us sit down upon them; then he took a piece of Cedar, which was full of little Round Holes, into one of which he thrust a stick of a harder substance than the Cedar, and began to rub it about pretty fast between the Palms of his Hands, till at length it took fire. The use he put it to was to light the Tobacco in his great Pipe; and after he had wept some time over us, and laid his Hands on our Heads, he made me smoak in a Calumet, or Pipe of Peace, and then acquainted us by Signs, that within sixteen days we should be at home (Hennepin 1699: 162).

After the party had finally reached Mille Lacs, and Hennepin was getting settled in his quarters, he described another weeping episode:

> At the entry of the Captain's cabin who had adopted me, one of the Barbarians, who seemed to be very old, presented me with a great Pipe to smoak in, and weeping over me all the while with abundance of Tears, rubb'd both my Arms and my Head. This was to show how concern'd he was to see me so harass'd and fatigu'd (Hennepin 1699: 168).

The Dakota elder who wept over Hennepin and who held a "great pipe" was no doubt a senior practitioner of Dakota Tradition and one who knew their history. It may be that the "great pipe" he carried was the pipe we know today as the Sacred Pipe of the Dakotas.

Hennepin was exhausted from the rapid pace of the Dakotas as they traveled to Mille Lacs; and to bring him back to health the Dakotas treated him with sweat baths and massage. Again they wept over him, as Hennepin described, "... and laying their hands on my body, began to rub it, and at the same time to weep bitterly" (Hennepin 1699: 170).

Hennepin would have had no idea that the Dakotas' extravagant weeping was like the medieval practice of the Cistercian monks and St. Bernard of Clairvaux at prayer. However, his next report plainly indicates that the Dakotas did see his appearance in the context of the source of their tradition. Hennepin's gear included his chasuble, which in Roman Catholic tradition is a sleeveless outer vestment worn by the celebrant at mass. Hennepin must have been dumbfounded when he observed the Dakotas using it in their ritual, which he described as follows:

> Aquipaguetin's Son, who call'd me Brother, had got my Brocard Chasuble, and was strutting up and down with it upon his naked Back. He had wrapp'd up in it the Bones of a Man who had been very considerable amongst them, for

whose Memory they had still a wonderful Respect. The Priest's Girdle which was made of red and white Wooll, with two Loops at the end serv'd him to fasten it, whilst he carry'd it up and down in Triumph, calling it Louis Chinnen, which signifies, as I since understand, the Robe of him, who is name'd the *Sun.* After they had for some time us'd my Chasuble as an Ornament to cover the Bones of their Dead, at the celebrating their most solemn Rites, they made a present of it to a People in Alliance with them, who liv'd 4 or 500 Leagues distant towards the West, but were come in Embassie, and had danc'd the Calumet (Hennepin 1699: 169).

Were the bones in Hennepin's chasuble those of Dakotas, or from ancient European visitors? Either way, the ceremony Hennepin observed was unique. If the bones were those of a Dakota ancestor, the ceremonial use of Hennepin's chasuble to carry Dakota bones indicates a very unusual merger of cultures, which under the circumstances seems very unlikely unless the Dakotas related Hennepin's presence to their Spiritual Tradition. It also may be possible that the bones were not Dakota, but were ancient relics usually stored in a tribal bundle that dated from the time of the KRS. There will be more speculation about the source and fate of those bones in a later chapter.

A major fact of Dakota history that is clearly established by Hennepin's account, is that although some Dakota Indians had already migrated west to the Great Plains prior to 1680, that those plains dwellers continued to maintain contact with the Dakotas back at Mille Lacs. We know this because Hennepin wrote that during his stay at Mille Lacs, four Indians, who must have been related Dakotas from the western plains, arrived there to visit. These were the same visitors to whom the Mille Lacs Dakota gave Hennepin's chasuble. That presentation indicates Dakota recognition of a relationship with the visitors, and that they shared some relationship with Hennepin. Why had the four visitors traveled east to Mille Lacs and why had they apparently done so in a hurried pace? Hennepin's account of the journey of these visitors to Mille Lacs is also interesting because it demonstrates that he had sufficient communication with them to write his detailed account; and it also shows that the Plains Dakotas were interested in him and sought him out. Those circumstances all are consistent with the hypothesis that the Dakotas, including those already living on the western Prairie, understood that the white man had some relevance to their Spiritual Tradition. Hennepin wrote about those visitors as follows:

> During my stay amongst the *Issati* and *Nadoussians*, there arriv'd four Savages in Embassie to these People. They had come about five hundred Leagues from the West; and told us by the Interpreters of the *Issati*, that they were four Moons upon the Way; for so it is they call their months. They added, that their Country was to the West, and that we lay to the East in respect of them; that they had march'd the whole time without resting, except to sleep, or kill Game for their Subsistence . . . and that in their whole Journey they had neither met with, nor passed over any *Great Lake*; by which Phrase they always mean the Sea, nor any Arm of it. . . . That none of the Nations within their Knowledge, who lie to the West and North-West of them, had any great Lake about their Countries, which were very large, but only Rivers, which coming from the North, run cross the Countries of their Neighbouring Nations, which border on their Confines . . . and that all the Nations which lie beyond their Country, and those which are next to them, do dwell in Meadows and large Fields, where are many wild Bulls. . . . The four Savages of the said Embassy assur'd us farther, that there were very few Forests in the Countries through which they pass'd in their way hither; insomuch that now and then they were so put to it for Fuel, that they were forced to make Fires of Bull's Dung, to boil

their Victuals with in Earthen Pots, which they make use of, as neither having, nor knowing of any better (Hennepin 1699: 176–8).

Obviously those visitors were well received by the Mille Lacs Dakota as evidenced by the fact that they participated in their host's sacred dances and Hennepin's chasuble was presented to them. The western visitors did not travel by horse. They could not have carried any significant amount of trade goods, so trade was not their purpose. The circumstances indicate that the visitors sought out Hennepin, again raising the question of, why? It also is clear from Hennepin's account, that from the onset the Plains Dakotas' destination had been Mille Lacs; they were not merely roaming the east. What could have prompted their effort? I believe that their trip was prompted because word had reached them that a white man, Du Luth, had visited their kinsmen at their ancient home at Mille Lacs. Because the Plains Dakota knew their history that told of the visit of the White Buffalo Woman in the fourteenth century at Mille Lacs, they were inspired to hurry east in hope of seeing the new white visitor for themselves. The Dakota legendary history of the ancient visit of white men (who they then called "Spirits") to their Spirit Lake was of such great significance to them, that the possibility that the event was now being repeated, was their motivation. In my view their journey tends to confirm that the ancient visitation by whites to Mille Lacs was a fact of history, not a myth.

Hennepin's account is clear evidence that the western prairie Dakota visitors thought that Hennepin did have a relationship with their cultural heritage; as shown by the fact that they used his garment in their ritual in the pipe (calumet) dance. Hennepin's chasuble was placed over the bones of the dead, and later presented to the four visitors from the western prairie as a gift. While Hennepin may not have appreciated the significance of that ceremonial dance, from the perspective of the Dakota it was a clear acknowledgment that Hennepin represented a connection with their spiritual tradition. What other reason would the Dakotas have to include Father Hennepin? The dance ceremony involving bones of the dead, that Hennepin saw and described, was a serious event for the Dakota, not sport or entertainment.

We also can interpret the arrival, in 1680, of the four western prairie Dakotas to Mille Lacs, as additional confirmation of the significance of Lake Mille Lacs to the Dakota. The very fact that it was their destination confirms its importance, and tends to confirm that it also would have been the place where any ancient European contact with the Dakotas would have taken place.

Hennepin's account of his Dakota contact also includes anecdotes indicating that his hosts believed that he had supernatural power, again suggesting that they connected him with their Spiritual Tradition. After Hennepin showed the Dakota chief Aquipaguetin, how his compass needle worked, the Chief told his people:

> ... that we were Spirits; and that we were capable of bringing things to pass that were altogether out of their power. At the end of his discourse all the elders wept over me, admiring in me things they could not comprehend (Hennepin 1699: 171).

Another example was Hennepin's recounting: "One day, seeing the Rain fall in such abundance, that they fear'd twould spoil their hunting, they order'd me to bid it cease" (Hennepin 1699: 173).

Hennepin began preparing a dictionary of his hosts' language and engaged the children in conversation in order to learn their words for various things, which he wrote down on paper. He recorded this account:

> Thus would they divert themselves with me, and often say to one another, *When we ask Father* Louis *anything,* (for they had heard our Canou-Men call me so) *he does not answer us.* But when he has lookt *upon the White,* (for they have no word for Paper) he *then talks, and makes us under-*

stand his Thoughts. This White thing, wou'd they add, *must needs be a Spirit, which teaches him to understand all we say* (Hennepin 1699: 172).

In a similar story, Father Hennepin wrote that he became aware that some Dakotas were wary or hostile to his reading from a book. In order to put their fears to rest he began singing from the book, describing it as follows:

Wherefore to use them to it by degrees, I was wont to sing the Litanies, as we were upon the Way, holding the Book in my hand. They fondly believed my Breviary was a Spirit which taught me to sing thus for their Diversion (Hennepin 1699: 164).

The Dakotas' lack of understanding of reading and writing in 1680, makes it easy to appreciate how their ancestors, some 318 years earlier, made the same error when they supposed the KRS was speaking when its inscription on the KRS was read aloud, giving rise to the Dakota notion that stones possessed supernatural power, including the ability to speak.

The Dakotas wondered if Hennepin, like the White Buffalo Woman, had come to teach and assist them. It is likely that the Kensington rune stone was covered in a "Issati" tribal bundle located somewhere in the Mille Lacs area when he was there. Perhaps it was shown to Hennepin, although he doesn't mention it. Hennepin took his leave from the Dakotas on good terms. They advised him on the best route, via the Wisconsin River, to reach Lake Michigan. The Dakotas may well have seen Hennepin's visit as confirmation of their Spiritual Tradition, and the record of Hennepin's interaction with the Dakotas offers confirmation that the Dakota Spiritual Tradition came from European sources.

The White Buffalo Woman
and the Sacred Pipe

THE CONTACT BETWEEN THE EUROPEAN MONKS who carved the KRS and the Dakota Indians in 1362 explains the origin of the story of the White Buffalo Woman and the Sacred Pipe. Black Elk told the story in his interviews with John G. Neihardt, who published it in *Black Elk Speaks* in 1932. Over a decade later another scholar, Joseph Epes Brown, lived with Black Elk and his family. Black Elk recounted his knowledge of Dakota Tradition to Brown, including a particularly detailed account of the White Buffalo Woman and her gift of the Sacred Pipe. Brown published these interviews in *The Sacred Pipe,* in 1953.

A summary of Black Elk's account as told to Brown is that a very beautiful woman, dressed in white, appeared. She asked that a large lodge be constructed for use during her visit. Her request was relayed back to Dakota leaders who ordered the lodge erected. In Black Elk's words: "the people were, of course, all very excited as they waited in the great lodge for the coming of the holy woman, and everybody was wondering where this mysterious woman came from and what it was that she wished to say" (Brown 1953: 4). Various versions of the story credit the White Buffalo Woman with teaching the Dakotas many positive, and Christian-like ideas. Black Elk said that when the woman presented the pipe she instructed them that it was to be used in seven rites which would be revealed to them. Black Elk described the woman as "holy, mysterious, strange, sacred and wakan." He also referred to her as the "White Buffalo Cow Woman" (Brown 1953: 11). Most versions of the story say that the woman became a White Buffalo Calf; which is why Dakota Indians regard an albino buffalo calf as sacred (Brown 1953: 9).

It is my hypothesis that one or more of the 14th century visiting monks taught Christianity to their Dakota hosts in much the same way as Christian missionaries have done for centuries in many parts of the world. What the Dakotas understood of that instruction about the Virgin Mary subsequently evolved into the story of the White Buffalo Woman.

The origin of the unusual name, White Buffalo Woman, is likely best explained by the fact that the explorers were the first white men that the Dakota had ever seen, and it was also the first time they had seen men with large bushy beards, that resembled the head of the buffalo. Following their practice of adopting names based on appearance, the Dakota probably called the explorers "white buffalo men." The monks who led the group of explorers very likely would have carried a portrait or statue of the Virgin Mary, portrayed as a beautiful white woman. It was a common medieval practice for a group to carry such an emblem or banner as they traveled, both to show to whom they gave their loyalty and devotion, and to invoke the protection of the holy person portrayed, in this case the Virgin Mary. Because the woman was carried by the White Buffalo Men, the Dakota saw her as the White Buffalo Woman.

Portraits were new to the Dakota and they probably regarded the portrait of the Virgin Mary as possessing some degree of life or power. The personification of the portrait would have been expanded in their minds in instances when the white buffalo men told the Dakota what the Virgin Mary wanted, or said. When the explorers indicated that they were carrying out the wishes of the Virgin Mary, it would give the Dakota reason to believe that she was in control and possessed power.

It is also important to remember that the whole theme of the White Buffalo Woman story and the Sacred Pipe which was given in her name is one of peace. While smoking pipes had been used by Indians long before 1362, the Sacred Pipe probably marks the point in Indian history where it became a symbol of peace, becoming known eventually as the calumet. Every version of the story of the Sacred Pipe reflects its peaceful origin.

Some writers have dismissed the evidence of Christian ideas in Dakota Indian tradition as the result of early post-Columbian Christian missionary activity. However the Dakotas did not have significant early missionary exposure. By the time missionaries came, their traditions were already established. The early missionaries were hostile to those Dakota traditions, which they labeled as superstitions, heathenism, paganism and devil worship. Now that very hostility to Dakota Spiritual Tradition has given way to reconciliation; and in the Roman Catholic Church in Dakota Indian areas, the White Buffalo Woman is identified with the Virgin Mary (Walker 1982: 14). That reconciliation has been based on obvious parallels and similarities, even though there was no understanding of where those parallels and similarities originated. Anthropologist Elaine A. Jahner, discussing the origins of the tradition of the White Buffalo Woman and the Sacred Pipe, wrote: "In terms of cosmic time, the events of the story are very recent indeed..." (Walker 1983: 52). Her insight was well taken. Now, thanks to our new understanding of the KRS, we can pinpoint the time of the introduction of the story to the Dakota Indians in 1362.

Wilbur A. Riegert viewed the Dakota Sacred Pipe in 1936, and was one of the first to suggest that the lady who gave the pipe and the Virgin Mary were the same (Riegert 1975: 120). Theological discussions aside, it seems clear that many observers have seen the similarity of the Dakota Spiritual Tradition and Christian teachings. It is my claim that those similarities exist because the origin of the Dakota traditions came from 14th century Christian teachings. The role of the Virgin Mary in Roman Catholic theology was at a high point during the 14th century, and nearly all new Church writing and hymns were about her. The Cistercian Order led in this practice, and it is easy to understand how a charismatic Cistercian teacher, teaching about the Virgin Mary, could have inspired the Dakota story of the White Buffalo Woman.

The Cistercians of today, like their predecessors, continue to emphasize the role of the Virgin Mary as a vital, caring, protective and potentially immediate presence. A modern statement of the role of Mary as understood today in the Cistercian Order is illustrative. M. Basil Pennington, in *Light from the Cloister* (1991), puts it this way: "I am conscious, as we begin to share, that the monastery is Mary's. She is here mothering us. . . . I place these pages, and you, dear Reader, into her loving hands" (Pennington 1991: 5). He also described the medieval Cistercian embrace of what he describes as "Marian piety," as follows:

> . . . they saw their monasteries as belonging to her as their Lady, the Mother and Consort of their Lord. All their monasteries bore her name, along with that of the locale: the Monastery of Blessed Mary of the Valley of Light (Clairvaux); the Monastery of Blessed Mary of the Beautiful Fountain (Bellefontaine), the Monastery of Blessed Mary of the Seven Fountains (Sept Fons). The monks— when they entered the monastic community and took up residence in her house—became her vassals and took her name, usually along with that of one of her great servants (Pennington 1991: 145).

The Dakotas usually tell the story of the White Buffalo Woman by describing her as a holy teacher, who taught them their Spiritual Tradition. That makes it clear that the Dakotas do not believe that their Spiritual Tradition evolved from within their culture from dreams or visions. Rather, they claim that it was taught to them by an outsider who was a stranger. Several Dakota sources place the time of the White Buffalo Woman's visit to have been in the 14th century, and place the locale of the visit in the Lake Mille Lacs region, the same place that I believe is described in the KRS inscription. The Dakota story is one of a visitation by a person dressed in white, presumably otherwise unknown to pre-Columbian Dakotas.

To understand how and why it was possible for Christian monks to have such a profound influence on the Dakotas in the 14th century, we must view the scene from the perspective of the Dakotas. The monks who would undertake such an exploration must have been vigorous individuals with positive attitudes. The European explorers, with their iron weapons, their craft skills and strongly held beliefs, would have impressed the Dakota Indians. Medieval Christians were not bothered by doubts or questions— they confidently accepted their faith and discounted any other. They had an absolutely positive perspective of their Christian faith, which would have left no room for doubt and likely gave them a dominating influence.

According to Susan Windgrow's account, the Nordic visitors remained over one winter (Landes 1968: 23). That long time provided an opportunity for them to exercise considerable influence. The large size of their party, their absolute dedication, their superior weapons, their good humor, their integrity, their advanced knowledge, and their ability to work with iron tools all would have contributed to the Dakota's strong and positive impression of their visitors.

Historian Royal B. Hassrick called the Dakota story of the White Buffalo Woman "a legend," although he acknowledged that the Dakotas believe the story to be factual. He noted their understanding that the woman had appeared to them over ten generations before (Hassrick 1964: 263).

Scholar Ruth Beebe Hill devoted 25 years to ethnographic study of the Dakota Indians which she turned into an historical novel, *Hanta Yo*, that tells a Dakota saga which took place from about 1769 to 1825. Early in the novel one of the characters tells the story of the White Buffalo Woman and says:

More than four hundred winters in the past, during a season of great unrest within the Dakotah family, something wonderful had happened. A woman had visited the tribe, bringing prophecy and a pipe—something to hold the people together ... (Hill 1979: 70).

Counting back 400 winters from 1769 takes one back to 1369, dating the time of the contact as calculated by Hill to a date remarkably close to the date of 1362 on the KRS. The Dakotas in Hill's study traced their paternal lineage to the Mdewakantonwan Dakota, who originated from the Lake Mille Lacs region where I believe the KRS was carved. The name that Hill chose for the ancestral Dakota father in her novel was Isantyati, a name which as I have shown elsewhere, refers to "cut stone."

There are three alternatives to understanding the story of the White Buffalo Woman. One choice is to accept it as told by Black Elk and others, as true in all details, including her transfiguration into a buffalo calf. No anthropologist has accepted that possibility so far as I can discover. A second choice is to see the story as a myth that evolved from visions or dreams or creative storytelling. It would appear that most anthropologists have held this view. While they have listened to their Dakota sources, and written respectfully, in their hearts I suspect they dismiss it all as myth. The myth explanation does not respect Dakota history and does not account for the existence of the Sacred Pipe. A third option, and the truth in my view, is that the story evolved out of a real event. The Dakotas met European monks exploring the west in 1362, and the Sacred Pipe was carved by one of those explorers who made a gift of it to the Dakotas in the name of the Virgin Mary.

Black Elk did not tell the account of the White Buffalo Woman as a folk tale or a vision. We can understand his statement to mean that it was an actual event in history. Black Elk was well aware of visions and dreams and knew their role in Dakota spiritual life; but he did not assign the story of the White Buffalo Woman to those traditions.

In his Dakota community Black Elk was also well known as a Christian leader. He was best known to his family and community as a dedicated and hardworking Catechist or lay priest. His conversion and work as a Catechist began more than 25 years before he was interviewed by Neihardt. By the time that Neihardt met him, Black Elk had completed assignments at five different Catholic churches and was well-known as a churchman. The most complete story of his life can be read in *Black Elk. Holy Man of the Oglala,* by Michael F. Steltenkamp. It is not the purpose of this book to assess the chronicles of Black Elk, but his story is important in solving the KRS mystery because Black Elk was probably the first person to have been steeped both in Dakota Spiritual Tradition and the Roman Catholic Church, and to reconcile those two presumably different faiths. When one realizes how the Dakota Spiritual Tradition originated, it is not difficult to understand how a thoughtful man like Black Elk, who knew and believed both traditions, could reconcile them to his own satisfaction. Similarly, Michael Steltenkamp, his biographer and a former Roman Catholic priest, also appears to accept this congruity of belief.

The location where Dakota tradition says that the White Buffalo Woman appeared was at Great Spirit Lake, or Mille Lacs. Some versions of the story say that she was first seen at a location a considerable distance from Mille Lacs and that messengers were sent on ahead to prepare a lodge for her. That scenario is consistent with the KRS inscription which says that the explorers left their ships in the care of ten men, by the sea which was 14 days' journey away. It is very unlikely that the Dakotas of the 14th century took instructions from either females or from strangers. Yet it is clear from many versions of the story that messengers were sent to tell of the arrival of the explorers and the White Buffalo Woman, their response was positive, and certainly not hostile.

Dakota tradition is that the pipe which the White Buffalo Woman presented to them still exists, and is kept in a tribal medicine bundle, under the supervision of a caretaker, in a small community called Green Grass, in South Dakota. The Sacred Pipe is not a myth or a vision. Steltenkamp wrote that the story of the White Buffalo Woman is the "ancient-Sioux equivalent to Judeo-Christian Scripture" (Steltenkamp 1982: 23). He is one of the few individuals who has personally viewed the Sacred Pipe. He also wrote that when the White Buffalo Woman came to the Dakotas that she said to them: "I do not wish to have any trouble with you because I am on a mission from God" (Steltenkamp 1982: 21).

The most important aspect of the Dakota story of the White Buffalo Woman, as they remember it today, is that she is the one who introduced the pipe, described by them as, "the gift of the pipe." The pipe was carved from Catlinite or pipestone. Presumably it was a pipe of a new design or style, which they could duplicate, and she instructed them how to do so. What could be a more likely gift and instruction, if the visitors were, as I believe, skilled stone craftsmen? It would have been easy for one of the European visitors, using a sharp iron tool, to fashion the pipe out of catlinite, and to give the Dakotas some tools so they could carve pipes themselves. Thus, the gift of the pipe. The wonderful climax to this story is that this very pipe, just like the Kensington rune stone, still exists. If the story of the White Buffalo Woman is merely a legend, who created the Sacred Pipe?

The Sacred Pipe is held by a caretaker. When Steltenkamp viewed the Sacred Pipe in 1976, some 614 years after 1362, he was told that the caretaker then in charge of the pipe was the nineteenth person to hold that honor (Steltenkamp 1982: 39). Dividing 614 years by 19 caretakers means approximately 32 years per caretaker. The role of caretaker may not have begun immediately after the pipe was first given, thus reducing the average time of service for each of the nineteen caretakers. With each caretaker serving for about 30 years on average, the pipe's 14th century time of origin is plausible.

Very few Dakota have ever viewed the Sacred Pipe. Many Dakotas who believe in the power of the pipe would not risk viewing it because they fear that they are not worthy to do so. Steltenkamp had the opportunity to view the pipe in 1976. He describes his trip for this viewing, and his preparation for the event, in considerable detail, in his 1982 book, *The Sacred Vision*. However, he avoids describing the pipe itself, even though the reason for his trip was to see the pipe. He also refers to the Sacred Pipe and its caretakers in his 1993 book, *Black Elk. Holy Man of the Oglala*, but again refrains from giving any description.

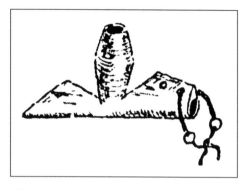

The Sacred Pipe.
The pyramidal forms in front of and behind the bowl are not otherwise known on pipes of this vintage. After a sketch from Sidney Thomas, "A Sioux Medicine Bundle," (1941).

What does the Sacred Pipe of the Dakotas look like? Does it have any features that would identify it as a European-inspired design? I believe that it does. The Dakota Sacred Pipe has been photographed. The photo was published together with an article about the pipe by Sidney J. Thomas, in *The American Anthropologist*, in 1941. The photographs and drawings show the Dakota Sacred Pipe to have three main features; the most prominent being a tall pipe bowl about in the middle, in a T shape. The unusual feature of the design is that there are two pyramid or triangular shaped projections, both about one half the height of the pipe bowl, one in front of the bowl and one to the rear. The rear pyramid is cut off at the end away from the bowl and has two holes through it where one could insert a cord. The surface of the pipe is smooth and without other markings. Thomas described the pipe as well finished catlinite or pipestone, but plain with no decoration by incision or bas-relief.

The medicine bundle that holds the Sacred Pipe of the Dakotas may well also hold other evidence proving the presence of medieval European visitors. The photographs in the 1941 Thomas article include a view of three unusual wooden objects that are kept in the bundle. Thomas described them as "Three wooden objects resembling ornate canoe paddles, highly polished and carefully made" (Thomas 1941: 606). Each is of a different design, about two feet long, carefully made. They do not appear to be tools or utensils. Because they are kept with the Sacred Pipe, it is possible that they are objects which were left behind by the 14th century visitors who created the Sacred Pipe. I have been unable to find any reference work that offers any aid in understanding the purpose for which those objects were made. Perhaps they are medieval craft tools possibly used for measuring, or aligning stone work, or that they were used in some way in church ceremonies or in monastic ritual. Hassrick wrote that the three wooden objects were "wooden paddles for ceremonially handling coals of fire" (Hassrick 1964: 260). However, he cites no authority for that idea and the description of the three objects in the Thomas article, which Hassrick cites, describes the wooden objects as "highly polished," and gives no hint that they had ever been exposed to hot coals. Probably the knowledge of the use intended for the wooden artifacts is long lost, however their true purpose may yet be discovered in some medieval European Church archive.

The prominent pyramid shapes featured on the Sacred Pipe do not represent common Dakota, or Native American shapes. A recent book, *Offering Smoke* (1988) by Jordan Paper, reviews the pipes of Native Americans with many illustrations. None of those illustrated have pyramid or triangular shaped projections. This suggests that the design of the Dakota Sacred Pipe is unique, and originated from outside sources. That, of course, is precisely what Black Elk repeatedly said.

Warren K. Moorhead prepared and published an exhaustive study in 1917 entitled, *Stone Ornaments Used by Indians in the United States and Canada.* His study did not include pipes, but did cover thousands of types and shapes of stone objects made by Native Americans. In no instance did he show any stone carved in what one could identify as a pyramid resembling those on the Sacred Pipe of the Dakotas. The pyramid was a common symbol of ancient stone masons, but it was not a common symbol of Native North America. In medieval Northern Europe the craft of stone masonry was a necessary part of the Catholic Church. They built the great cathedrals and thousands of monasteries. Cistercian monks were often stone masons and constructed their own monasteries and churches. Probably the design of the Dakota Sacred Pipe was the inspiration of one of them.

Some accounts of the Dakota White Buffalo Woman story say that she was mystically transfigured into a white buffalo calf, and in some versions, she then joined the vast buffalo herds of the prairies. Many references to the story use the word "calf" rather than woman, so today the Dakota Sacred Pipe is often referred to as the Sacred Calf Pipe. It is precisely that transfiguration legend that adds significance to the discovery of a buffalo calf skeleton buried in the Fingerson mound, the same mound where ten left femora were once buried by the Dakota Indians. This is the mound described in the chapter on the transport and burial of the KRS. It is located only about 18 miles southeast of where the KRS was discovered. Even today, the Dakota see the birth of an albino buffalo calf as a special and sacred event. The fact that a complete buffalo calf, except for the head, was buried in a mound near where the KRS was found suggests some relationship between the two burials.

Some accounts of the White Buffalo Woman story include an incident where she was first met by two young Dakota males, and that one of them was so taken with her beauty that he contemplated a sexual advance or assault, whereupon he was immediately struck dead. This incident may have originated because one of the Dakotas, who had been in close association with the visitors, died suddenly from the plague, just as did the ten members of the exploring party. Medieval Europeans commonly believed that the plague was punishment by God for sin; so probably the visiting monks advised the Dakotas that their young man's sudden death was punishment for sin. The Dakota's death would have seen as proof in the minds of the monks, that the deceased had been guilty of evil thoughts. On the other hand, from the perspective of the Dakotas, the sudden death of the young man served to demonstrate the power of the White Buffalo Woman.

When one appreciates the significance of the story of the White Buffalo Woman, one can understand why they were overjoyed when Pierre Esprit Radisson, a Frenchman, along with his brother-in-law, Médard Chouart, Sieur des Groseilliers, camped for the winter on the south shore of Lake Superior. Dakota Indians welcomed them and wept tears of joy over them. They then escorted the pair westerly to a location near Lake Mille Lacs, where they proceeded to construct what Radisson described as a fort. It was of enormous size, an enclosure of about 40 acres according to Radisson's account. Masses of visiting Dakotas gathered for a tumultuous welcome. Part of Radisson's description was:

> . . . they arrived with an incredible pomp. This made me think of the entrance that the Polanders did in Paris, saving that they had not so many jewels, but instead of them they had so many feathers . . . they have a white robe made of castors skins painted . . . the elders came with great gravity and modesty . . . Everyone had in his hand a pipe of council (Radisson 1961: 137).

Why would the supposed warlike Dakota Indians stage such a joyous ceremonial welcome for two half starved Europeans? The reason, I believe, was their mistaken notion that Radisson and Groseilliers somehow represented a return of white explorers like those who had brought the White Buffalo Woman to them in the distant past. Their spontaneous undertaking to construct a large fort or enclosure for their visitors, recalls the Dakota's preparation of a lodge for the visit of the White Buffalo Woman. The location selected by the Dakotas to erect Radisson's "fort" may well have been the same site where the 14th century visitors had taught the Dakotas, and where the painted image or statue of the Virgin Mary had stood in 1362.

From Knife Lake
to Kensington

C ONCLUDING, AS I HAVE, THAT THE KRS WAS CARVED
in the Lake Mille Lac region, most likely on an island in
nearby Knife Lake, leads to new questions. Why and
how did it come up to be buried on a small hilltop in Douglas
county, Minnesota, many miles to the west? The answer to why is
easy. The Dakota Indians moved to the west from the Lake Mille
Lacs region over a period of several centuries. At one point during that time one of the Dakota tribes believed that the KRS was
an important mystical or spiritual object, and so took it with them
when they left. Just how and when that happened is the next
riddle of the KRS story.

We can be sure that the KRS was intentionally buried and
would not have merely settled into the ground because frost action in Minnesota, where the frost goes down deep in winter,
forces stones upward. Also the reports that the stone was held in
the roots of a tree means that the stone was below the tree and so
must have been underground for a long time.

The most recent evidence that also confirms the fact that the
KRS had been buried for a long time prior to its discovery has just
been published by Barry J. Hanson, an investigator who arranged
to have the KRS examined by scanning electron microscopy at
Iowa State University, in Ames. Hanson reports that the tests
show that the KRS has been buried for a minimum period of fifty,
and probably as many as 200 years after it was carved (Hanson

2001: 80). The test result showing that the KRS was buried well before 1848 eliminates any possibility of forgery because Douglas county was then unsettled territory. That county was not organized until 1858. None of the "usual suspects" claimed to have been the forgers were yet born in 1858, or were only children living far from Douglas county. The Dakota migration west began over 200 years before the discovery date of 1898 so the entire range of the years covered by test results are within that period. While some of the possible explanations for its burial by the Dakota could date back to 1698, it may also be that the test results showing its burial for that long a time reflect the way the KRS was stored or kept for safekeeping in conditions similar to burial in the ground. The test results finally answer all claims of forgery and leave open only the questions of who carved the inscription, where, who carried it west, who buried it, and why.

The fact that the discovery site was a remote location that had no relationship to the geographic references in the inscription has always been a major obstacle to its acceptance as authentic. Hjalmar R. Holand, who saved the KRS from obscurity, crafted an explanation based on his assumption that the inscription had been carved where the KRS was found. This effort was seen by many as a house of cards that invited ridicule. On the other hand, what the critics of the KRS's authenticity have failed to appreciate is that it makes little sense to attempt a hoax using references that do not fit the site.

At least one historian has suggested that the stone was buried by the Dakota Indians. Farley Mowat wrote that "the place where the stone was left by the Norse need not have been the place where it was found. It could have been discovered by Indians and taken away by them. Considered as a cult object, it could have remained in their hands for years or even for generations, and it may have been carried a considerable distance from its original site" (Mowat 1965: 300). I believe that Mowat was correct about Indians transporting the stone and later burying it, but he did not grasp the fact that the inscription told of the Black Death. He also did not try to locate the sites described in the inscription, or to consider the vocation of its authors.

Many details of the Dakota Indian western migration from the Mille Lacs area to the Great Plains are lost to history. Clearly it occurred over a period of several hundred years. When was the KRS carried west? Which Dakotas possessed and carried the stone? Which route eventually led to the stone's burial site? Why was it buried? None of these questions may ever be definitively answered, however, the historical record provides several plausible answers.

Prior to the late nineteenth century the area that is now eastern central Minnesota, including the Mille Lacs region, was covered by a mature dense pine forest. The abundance of fish and wild rice at Lake Mille Lacs probably furnished more food than was usually available in most Indian communities. This abundance led to population expansion and overcrowding which may have induced some to leave for the more open spaces to the west.

While Lake Mille Lacs abounded with fish, the mature pine forest would not have been a particularly good habitat for deer, buffalo, and other large game, because the mature forest does not offer the new growth that provides food for big game. The Great Plains began about one hundred miles west of Mille Lacs, and between the plains and the pine forest was a wide transition zone with a mixed environment of grasslands, lakes and streams, and forests of deciduous trees. Prairie grass fires were often pushed east by the prevailing westerly winds into the transition zone, clearing areas where new growth would then emerge. It was a habitat of mixed vegetation where deer and other game could thrive. The transition zone was a prime hunting area for the Indians, and the KRS was buried in a central location in that transition zone.

There were two main waterway routes used by the Dakota Indians to reach this prime hunting zone. When they lived in the Mille Lacs area they used the Long Prairie River which begins in Douglas county from a chain of lakes, and flows east to the

Mississippi River. It is very likely that some groups of Dakota Indians, when migrating west, also used that river route to travel west by water as far as possible, and then continued overland to the western prairies. There is also an old overland trail that more or less parallels that water route, which was probably used by Indians when traveling in large groups. That overland route later was known as the Wadsworth Trail because it was used to reach Fort Wadsworth, later renamed Fort Sissiton, which was located in Dakota Territory. After the Ojibway Indians occupied the Mille Lacs area in about 1750, they also used the same Long Prairie River route to reach the transition zone for big game hunting.

The other route used by the Dakota Indians to reach what is now Douglas county was from the south. After about 1750 all of the Dakota Indians had left the Mille Lacs area and many had moved south to sites along the Mississippi River in the area where Minneapolis and St. Paul are now located. That is also where the Minnesota River enters the Mississippi. The Minnesota (formerly St. Peter's River) begins in the west from a lake on the Minnesota and South Dakota border and flows east to the Mississippi. This was a natural route for the Dakotas to follow to the western prairie. Many of the Dakotas moved west and established settlements along the Minnesota River. The Dakotas living at those Minnesota River locations continued to hunt in the Douglas county area. They were able to reach it by traveling north on what is now called the Chippewa River, following it upstream from where it enters the Minnesota River to its beginnings in various wetland areas of Douglas county.

The KRS was found in Douglas county in an area approximately midway between where the Long Prairie and Chippewa waterway routes both originate. Because both streams begin in the same area, this enabled the Dakota and Ojibway to use those river routes to mount attacks on each other, as well as to hunt. An account from an early local history of Douglas county describes it this way:

This particular locality was a favorable hunting ground for the redmen, and as they moved frequently about the country they established certain well defined paths leading from one camping ground to another. As this was a part of the ground where the Chippewas and the Sioux had frequently bloody encounters, these trails were often traveled by war parties of one or another tribe (Larson 1916: 427).

Doane Robinson wrote in *A History of the Dakota or Sioux Indians* that:

> At this period (1760–1800) ... the favorite hunting grounds of the Sissetons and Wahpetons (Dakotas) were about Long Prairie and Alexandria, (the County Seat of Douglas county) and in the progress of time the Chippewas began to resort to the same locality, and these meetings were usually attended by more or less bloodshed, though it happened more than once when the enemies were about of equal strength that they made a peace and hunted quietly together the game, which in the timber surrounding this prairie abounded in greater abundance than elsewhere (Robinson 1904: 65).

It is possible to suggest several reasonable scenarios to explain how it came to be that the Dakotas buried the KRS where they did. The most straightforward explanation is that a party of Dakotas, while still living near Mille Lacs, decided to move west and take the KRS with them. They would have followed the Wadsworth Trail, or traveled via the Long Prairie River to the chain of lakes in Douglas county, followed those lakes south, and then continued their journey west on foot. Perhaps after they had traveled overland for some time, the 200 pound KRS proved to be a great burden, and so they decided to hold an appropriate ceremony and bury it for safekeeping, intending to return and reclaim it in the future. To help them find it in the future, they marked the place by transplanting an aspen tree over the stone.

For some reason the stone was never recovered, and over the years that followed the aspen tree marking the burial place of the KRS may have been destroyed by fire, but because its roots survived the fire, a new tree sprouted to replace the old, and so the aspen continued to mark the site.

This first scenario suggests an early Dakota migration to the west. Two Dakota groups which are thought to have been the earliest migrants west were the Tetons and the Assiniboine. Possibly one those groups carried the KRS. Missionary Stephen Riggs, quoting a missionary from Saskatchewan, wrote "The name Assinaboine means Stone Sioux, and is a compound of French and Ojibwa . . . These Stoneys are said to be all Christians" (Riggs 1880: 277, 278). Perhaps their name of stone came from a tradition that they once possessed the KRS. By the 1870's the Assiniboine were living in Saskatchewan, Canada. It is possible that their assimilation into Christianity came about because they were able to see its parallels to their traditions, which had emerged out of their fourteenth century European Christian contact; and so like Black Elk, many years later, they accepted the two traditions as essentially non-contradictory. Another Dakota group, the Gros Ventres, may also have been early migrants from Mille Lacs. When first met by post-Columbian explorers they lived on the Missouri River near the Mandan Indians. One hint that they could have once possessed the KRS is the tradition that they had some ancient relationship to the Ojibway, who we will see also played an important role in the story of the KRS.

A second possibility to explain the burial of the KRS in Douglas county is that it was buried by the Dakotas during the Sioux Uprising in 1862, as part of their ritual in preparing for battle. Accounts from the Uprising report that the Dakotas spent many hours in ceremonies before attacking. Many of the Dakotas saw the Uprising as their last chance to reverse their Nation's fate. To demonstrate their dedication, they may have invoked the power of their most important mystical object, the KRS, to aid in their cause. Douglas county was on the western edge of settlement and there was considerable Dakota Indian activity noted in that area during the Uprising, frightening many settlers in the area into abandoning their homes. Troops were stationed for some time in Alexandria, where a fort was quickly constructed. The 1862 date, thirty-six years before the KRS was found, would have allowed enough time for the Aspen tree, placed over the KRS by the Dakotas as part of their ceremony, to grow to the size reported when the stone was found.

A third explanation for the KRS burial in Douglas county, and the one which I think is most likely to have been the case, is that it was abandoned in a farewell ceremony by the Dakotas who possessed it because they had been converted to Christianity by missionaries. Dakota history records numerous instances where Dakota Indians buried objects that they once held sacred, after they had become convinced that their old beliefs were false. This hypothesis postulates that the Dakotas carried the KRS with them when they left the Mille Lacs and Knife Lake area, moved south to the Mississippi River, and resided in the area where St. Paul is now located. In 1766, when the Dakotas were visited there by Jonathan Carver, I believe that he was shown the KRS. The story of his contact with the Dakotas and the KRS is considered in the next chapter. Subsequently many of the Dakotas moved west, including the group who possessed the KRS, and they resided in various locations along the Minnesota River.

The early name for the Minnesota River was St. Peter's River, however that name was derived originally from the French for stone, which is pierre, making it Stone River, which evolved to St. Peter's River, and later changed to the Minnesota River. It has fewer stones, or stone formations, than one might expect to see in a river, and is relatively free of rapids. It may be that the original name, Stone, referred to a particular stone, the KRS.

The Dakota Indian practice of burying objects that they had once believed to be sacred, but later wished to discard after exposure to white teaching, was the Dakotas' method of closure; and that practice has been recorded by various observers or scholars.

One of the earliest accounts was written by the frontier artist, George Catlin, in the 1830's, as follows:

> The word medicine, in its common acceptation here means *mystery* and nothing else . . .

> The "medicine-bag" then, is a mystery-bag . . . These bags are constructed of the skins of animals, of birds, or of reptiles, and ornamented and preserved in a thousand different ways . . . I find that every Indian in his primitive state, carries his medicine-bag in some form or other, to which he pays the greatest homage, and to which he looks for safety and protection through life . . .

> This curious custom has principally been done away with along the frontier, where white man laugh at the Indian for the observance of so ridiculous and useless a form; but in this country [along the Missouri River] it is in full force, and every male in the tribe carries this, his supernatural charm or guardian, to which he looks for the preservation of his life, in battle or in other danger; at which times it would be considered ominous of bad luck and an ill fate to be without it . . .

> The value of the medicine-bag to the Indian is beyond all price; for to sell it, or give it away, would subject him to such signal disgrace in his tribe, that he could never rise above it; and again, his superstition would stand in the way of any such disposition of it, for he considers it the gift of the Great Spirit . . .

> During my travels thus far, I have been unable to buy a medicine-bag of an Indian, although I have offered them extravagant prices for them; and even on the frontier, where they have been induced to abandon the practice, though a white man may induce an Indian to relinquish his medicine, yet he cannot *buy* it of him—the Indian in such

case will bury it, to please a white man, and save it from his sacrilegious touch; and he will linger around the spot and at regular times visit it and pay it his devotions, as long as he lives (Catlin 1841: 35–37).

Just as individual Indians had medicine bags, so did the tribe have its medicine bundle, and just as individuals buried their medicine bags, tribal medicine bundles were buried by Plains Indians after Christian teachers had persuaded them that the bundles were cult objects (Landes 1970: 43).

My hypothesis is that the KRS was held by a Dakota Indian group in what was essentially a tribal medicine bundle. It was a pagan cult object as far as the frontier Christian missionaries were concerned, and they required the Indians to give up their old beliefs and its paraphernalia before accepting them into Christian church membership.

Within the limitations of this book it is difficult to adequately describe the major impact on the Dakota Indians who were taught by a number of the Christian missionaries who lived and worked along the Minnesota River beginning in 1834 until 1862. The leader of that effort was Thomas S. Williamson. In 1834, Fort Snelling, where Minneapolis-St. Paul are now located, was an isolated, remote U. S. Army outpost, accessible mainly via the Mississippi River from the rest of the Nation. The Williamson mission, established in 1835, was about 150 miles west of Fort Snelling, on the Minnesota River. Williamson's family was also dedicated to the cause, and he was joined by a number of others, the most well-known being Stephen R. Riggs and his wife, Mary, mentioned earlier for their work on a Dakota dictionary. Their influence is important to the story of the KRS because it is my view that it was their teaching that eventually prompted the Dakotas who possessed the KRS to bury it where it was later found. A considerable number of Dakota were converted to Christianity and enrolled as members of the church. Admission of the Dakotas into church membership was not a casual matter

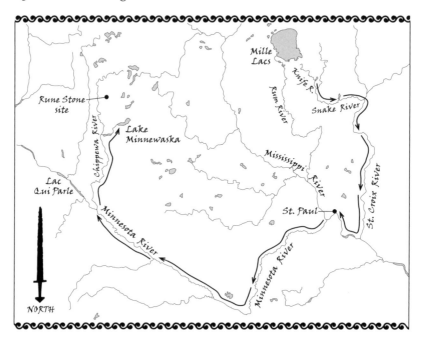

From Knife Island, where the KRS was carved, the rune stone's long journey eventually ended at Olof Ohman's farm.

in the 1840s. They were only enrolled after being tested on the sincerity of their belief and their knowledge of the faith, and only if they met high standards of moral behavior. These rigorous standards necessarily required Dakota converts to give up their old beliefs and the objects that related to their old practices. The missionaries were urging the Dakotas to make a complete change of culture and to take up farming for a livelihood, to become assimilated into the white population. Because of the efforts of those missionaries many Sissiton and Wahpeton Dakota who had been converted or influenced, refused to join in the Sioux Uprising in 1862, and instead saved the lives of many white settlers by taking them under their protection, or by warning them of pending danger in time to make their escape (Willard 1964: 237).

During their conversion, those Dakotas had been faced with the need to discard the KRS to qualify for admission to the mission church. It is my opinion that they did so by burying it in the same manner that other Dakotas had buried their medicine bags, as described by George Catlin. They carried the KRS north on the Chippewa River to their prime hunting grounds. The Dakota name for the Chippewa River was Maya Wakan, meaning a "steep place," and wakan meaning "Spirit or something consecrated" (Riggs 1852: 137, 214). The Dakota name certainly implies that they believed this river had special significance. Probably the Dakotas then followed various Chippewa River tributaries and adjacent wetland areas to some point near the KRS discovery site, and carried the stone the final distance to where they buried it near the top of a hill. They bade it farewell in a respectful manner and planted an aspen tree over the stone in the manner of their old tradition, and also to mark the burial place. One of the reasons why I think that the KRS was buried sometime in the 1840s is because of the apparent age and root configuration of the aspen tree that marked the burial site of the stone when it was found in 1898. I think that the Dakotas had selected and dug up a small aspen sapling and placed its roots directly over the stone when they buried it, so that the aspen's roots naturally embraced the stone as the tree grew in the years thereafter. Most likely the Dakotas who buried the KRS kept their secret. With their deaths, their people lost track of the cut stone that had inspired much of the Dakota ancient tradition. The presence of the aspen tree was the only reason why the KRS was ever discovered.

There are several plausible reasons why the Dakotas carried the KRS from the Minnesota River area as far north as the Douglas county area before burying it. One reason may have been that they wished to carry it as far back as possible toward their ancient homelands at Mille Lacs and Knife Lake without risking conflict with the Ojibway Indians. A second reason could have been that they continued to regard the KRS with considerable awe, and so they wished to bury it far from where they lived to lessen the risk that the stone might exert its mystic power over them. A third reason may have been to bury it in their prime hunting area so that they could revisit the site when on hunting trips in the future. A fourth reason may have been that they sought to bring the KRS into the vicinity of group of high hills that the Dakotas regarded as mystic, known as the Leaf Hills, a little known group of hills in northern Douglas county and southern Otter Tail county. These hills afforded long vistas and had large growths of aspen trees, usually rustling with the slightest breeze. The Leaf Hills were particularly the haunt of the Wahpeton or Leaf Dakotas, a tribe from which the Williamson and Riggs' mission was most successful in making converts to Christianity beginning in about 1837 (Riggs 1890: 54). The relative ease with which the missionaries converted the Wahpeton Dakotas suggests that they were the Dakota who buried the KRS. The KRS was buried some miles south of the Leaf Hills, but the Dakotas may have had them as their destination but for some reason stopped short of that goal. A fifth reason may have been that they wanted to carry the stone far from the mission so that their burial ceremony would not be seen by the missionaries. A sixth reason may be that they initially intended to bury the KRS in an old mound (the Fingerson mound) that was located about 18 miles southeast of the eventual burial site, but for some reason they changed their plans, and instead continued north to the KRS site.

Catlin wrote that even though the Dakotas abandoned their mystic objects by burying them, that nevertheless former owners would return from time to time to visit the burial site. Possibly the same idea was in the minds of those who buried the KRS. The practice of Dakota Indians returning from time to time to visit sites where they had previously buried objects of mystery was noted and recorded in respect to the Fingerson mound, a Dakota mound that was located only about 18 miles southeast of the KRS discovery site. When archaeologists studied that site in 1938, their inquiries produced the information that: "The older inhabitants of the area reported that in pioneer days the Sioux Indians showed much interest in this mound and often visited it in small groups" (Wilford, Johnson, Vicinus 1969: 42). The Fingerson mound was on the south shore of Lake Minnewaska, in Pope county, which is south of and adjacent to Douglas county; and would also have been reached by Dakota Indians who lived along the Minnesota River via the Chippewa River. Fantastic as it may seem, the bones found in 1938, in the Fingerson mound may relate to the KRS.

Many Indian mounds have been identified in Minnesota which undoubtedly were built by the forefathers of the Dakota Indians; however, archaeological analysis shows that Dakota mound building ended several hundred years before post-Columbian contact. After mound building ceased, the existing old mounds were sometimes used for secondary burials, meaning that bones which had been collected from bodies that had been placed on scaffolds might later be reburied in mounds. The Fingerson mound, excavated in 1938, yielded unusual individual bones buried there in secondary burials. The remarkable aspect of the Fingerson mound was that, while the aggregate quantity of human bones that were found were so few that together they added up to less than one individual, the site also contained ten human bones, each one of which was identified as an adult left femur—which is the long single bone between the hip and knee. Eight were found together in one grouping and two in another. Obviously those ten left femora had come from ten different individuals, and had been deliberately selected and preserved elsewhere, for perhaps a long time, before being deposited in the mound. A possible explanation for that unique collection of ten left femora could be that they came from the bodies of the ten explorers whose deaths were recorded in the KRS inscription. It may be that those ten left femora had been preserved and carried in the same tribal medicine bundle that contained the KRS, and were buried at, or about the same time that the KRS was buried, only in the nearby Fingerson mound. It is also possible that those ten left femora were the same bones of the dead that Hennepin, in 1680, saw the Dakotas carry in his chasuble and feature in their dance before him.

Modern day forensic science might have been able to settle the question of whether or not those ten left femora were of European or Indian origin—but it appears that the bones found in the Fingerson mound are now lost for study because they were reburied after recent changes in the law prohibited archaeological retention of human bones. In 1994 the Smithsonian Institution published a 32 chapter collection of studies entitled: *Skeletal Biology in the Great Plains,* containing chapters on Northern and Southern Plains femora by Theodore M. Cole, III and Christopher Ruff. It seems clear that considerable data on Dakota Indian femora does exist. If field notes or other records of the ten femora that were found in the Fingerson mound could be located, the question of their origin may yet be determined.

The idea that the left femur of each of the deceased explorers would have been preserved seems bizarre today, however a major aspect of 14th century European Christian practice was to preserve the bones of the dead in an ossuary—which literally was a place where bones of the dead were stored and sometimes displayed. An ossuary church was sometimes built next to the main church. The medieval Christian ossuary practices are now rarely mentioned, presumably because by today's thinking they are embarrassingly "medieval," however, we must remember that the KRS was carved in 1362, and is medieval. Perhaps the largest Christian ossuary still extant, was founded by the Cistercian order, and has been preserved in Sedlec, Bohemia. It appears that beginning in the thirteenth century the site became identified as a particularly desirable place of final rest so many thousands of bodies were brought there from all over Europe. Eventually the Cistercian property at Sedlec passed into non-church ownership, and in 1870 the owner employed artists who used the bones from about 40,000 people to decorate the ossuary as it survives today. The remaining other bones, comprising about 40 cubic meters, were buried in the ground. Preserving the bones of dead martyrs or saints in glass coffins or reliquaries, where they can be seen and honored, is a practice that continues today at certain places in the Roman Catholic Church.

Medieval Christians believed it was vital to be buried in holy ground, which was not possible if one died at a place where holy ground was not available, such as while exploring an unknown country. A partial solution could have been to carry some bones of the deceased back to holy ground for proper burial. When ten members of the KRS exploring party died, the issue of burial in holy ground confronted the surviving Cistercian monks. They may have solved that problem by determining to carry back some bones of the deceased; and this necessitated allowing the bodies to decompose so that the bones could be recovered. My speculation is that this was done by placing the bodies on scaffolds. It is my further speculation that the Dakotas observed this unusual activity by their visitors and so concluded that it was the proper way to care for the dead; and so they adopted the practice for themselves. Without digressing too far, it seems clear from archaeological studies that for centuries the Dakota Indians had built mounds where they buried their dead. However, in about the 14th century they discontinued mound burials, built no more mounds, and adopted the practice of scaffold burial where they placed the bodies of the dead on a scaffold until the bones could be recovered, and then retained in bundles. These bundles sometimes were buried in intrusive burials in old mounds, of which there were thousands. While pointing to a specific cause is speculative, it is well established that this abrupt shift in Dakota funerary practice occurred in the medieval period, and also that scaffold burials were unique to the Dakotas. There must have been some significant reason for that change, but until now, no reason was known. That change coincides with the other changes in Dakota perspective and tradition that occurred at that time.

As to the ten left femora that archeologists found in the Fingerson mound in 1938, it may have been the case that the monks found themselves too heavily laden when they made ready to leave the Dakotas in 1363, so they had to leave some of the bones they had recovered in the care of their hosts, possibly to be recovered on a later visit. According to Susan Windgrow's account of

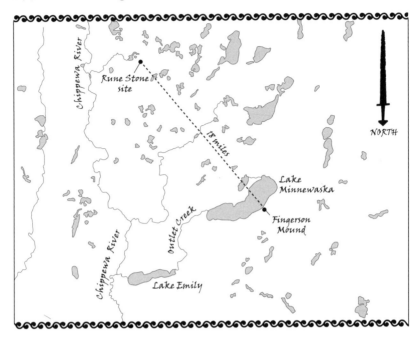

Both the Fingerson mound and KRS site can be reached from the south via the Chippewa River.

Europeans visiting Mystic Lake, recorded by Ruth Landes, when the visitors departed they promised to return. Because they never returned, the Dakotas assumed that they had met death elsewhere (Landes 1968: 23). The Dakotas' recollection of that history would explain why, in 1680, the Dakotas placed human bones in Hennepin's white chasuble and featured them in a ceremony in Hennepin's presence. Perhaps they expected that he would know the origin of the bones and reclaim them. Of course, Hennepin assumed that the bones were those of a deceased Dakota Indian. Why would the Dakotas involve Hennepin, a white man, a stranger and an outsider, with the bones of their ancestors? Whether or not they were the same bones mentioned in Hennepin's account, it is clear that the ten left femora found in the Fingerson mound were an unusual collection of bones, and one whose unique nature calls for an answer. It seems odd that no one has noticed that the number of left femurs found in the Fingerson mound was the same as the number of dead mentioned on the KRS, however when experts assume a hoax, it limits their vision.

Other archaeological findings in the Fingerson mound reveal that it was a place where the Dakota Indians engaged in rites similar to rituals described by Black Elk. The site included a rock cairn of twenty rocks, the largest being at the bottom. Remains of the ends of nine wooden poles were found, some preserved so that the grain of the wood could be seen, with the largest placed vertically near the center. The description of the cairn resembles the altar hole filed with rocks which Black Elk described, and the remains of the nine poles suggest that some apparatus had been erected there similar to the sun dance construction. Enough remained of the pole to be identifiable by archaeologists in 1938.

The other human bones found in the Fingerson mound were described as a few calcined human bones reduced to very small white fragments. These, found at 1.25 feet above the original surface level and 1 foot below the mound surface, led the archaeologists to conclude that they had been calcined elsewhere and deposited in a shallow excavation in the mound after its construction (Wilford, Johnson and Vicinus 1969: 42). Perhaps they also relate to the 14th century.

That same Fingerson mound also contained remarkable evidence relating to the Dakota Spiritual Tradition story of the White Buffalo Woman, as it contained the skeleton of a bison calf in perfect anatomical position that was complete except for the head (Wilford, Johnson and Vicinus 1969: 42). Many versions of the White Buffalo Woman legend say that she turned into a white buffalo calf, and then joined the massive buffalo herds on the Great Plains. Her transformation into a Buffalo is one reason why the word "Buffalo" is part of her name. That legend persists and the birth of an albino bison calf is today still seen as a significant event in Dakota Indian culture. It seems very likely that the headless skeleton of a bison calf was that of an albino, and that is why it was carefully buried in the mound.

New information about the Fingerson mound was announced

by David Mather in November, 2000, at the joint Midwest Archaeological/Plains Anthropological Conference. In his paper, entitled "The Headless Bison Calf from the Fingerson Mound, Pope County, Minnesota," Mather reviewed the Sonota Complex, thought to date from A.D. 1 to 450, a time period that some had believed included the Fingerson mound. As part of his research, Mather obtained a radio carbon date of one of the bones of the buffalo calf and received the results back only a few days before the conference. The bone could only be dated after 1670.

The fact that the skeleton of the bison calf, the ten left femora, and the ceremonial stone cairn were all found in the same mound, located only about 18 miles from where the KRS was buried, suggest that the Dakotas saw them as significant and related artifacts. The late radio carbon date is consistent with the Wilford, Johnson and Vicinus report that early settlers told of Dakota Indians visiting the Fingerson mound from time to time. The Dakota Indians were obviously making ceremonial burials near where the Kensington stone was buried, probably between 1830 and 1862. Both the KRS site and the Fingerson mound lie in the area of the headwater streams or creeks that merge into the Chippewa River, which means that Dakotas heading north to those sites would follow the same route until very close to either site.

In earlier consideration of the KRS, Holand and other advocates for its authenticity assumed that it was carved and placed where it was discovered. Soon after it was carved, they felt that it had toppled over and eventually became covered by soil, and that eventually an aspen tree chanced to grow over the stone. As part of his effort to establish the veracity of the witnesses to the stone's discovery, Holand arranged for them to make affidavits describing the event. While Holand's purpose in securing the affidavits was to support the proposition that those who found the KRS were truthful, it is my view that the facts of the discovery that are given in those affidavits also are consistent with my hypothesis that the KRS had been purposefully buried, and that the aspen tree was intentionally placed over the stone by the people who buried it.

In his affidavit, Olof Ohman, the farmer who unearthed the KRS, stated:

Upon removing an asp, [aspen] measuring about 10 inches in diameter at its base, I discovered a flat stone inscribed with characters, to me unintelligible. The stone laid just beneath the surface of the ground in a slightly slanting position, with one corner almost protruding. The two largest roots of the tree clasped the stone in such a manner that the stone must have been there at least as long as the tree. One of the roots penetrated directly downward and was flat on the side next to the stone. The other root extended almost horizontally across the stone and made at its edge a right angled turn downward. At this turn the root was flattened on the side toward the stone. This root was about three inches in diameter (Holand 1932: 34).

Ohman's next door neighbor, Nils Flaten, who was called over to see the rune stone after it was found, affirmed:

The two largest roots of the asp were flattened on their inner surface and bent by nature in such a way as to exactly conform to the outlines of the stone (Holand 1932: 36).

Ohman's son, Edward, was 10 years old when the KRS was found and was with his father in the field when the KRS was unearthed. Eleven years later he described the event in an affidavit, as follows:

... in removing an asp, a stone was found imbedded in the ground and embraced by two roots of said asp, one root going downward on one side of the stone and so close to it that its surface was flattened from contact; the other root pursuing a nearly horizontal course across the surface of the stone, where it bent down into the ground, forming a right angle. The stump of the asp was about ten inches in diameter at the base, the horizontal root about three inches in diameter. I saw the stone in the ground, and the roots in their undisturbed position on the side and surface of the stone. After my father had got the stone out of the ground, and we had rolled it to one side, I noticed that some characters were inscribed on the stone and called my father's attention to it (Holand 1932: 294).

Ohman's neighbor Nils Flaten, who could see the hill where the rune stone was discovered from his house, included the fact that the aspen tree over the KRS was surrounded by underbrush, which indicates that the tree was not part of a grove of aspen, but stood alone. The solitary tree also suggests that it had been intentionally placed at that site. Flaten affirmed:

I had visited the same spot earlier in the day before Mr. Ohman had cut down the tree and also many times previously—but I had never seen anything suspicious there. Besides the asp, the roots of which embraced the stone, the spot was also covered by a very heavy growth of underbrush (Holand 1932: 36).

It seems clear that unless those affidavits were all lies, the KRS was held within the aspen tree's roots, and had been underground at that site for many years.

The fact that the KRS was found encased in the roots of an aspen tree, is an important clue to identifying who buried it because the aspen is the tree which the Dakota prescribe for their ceremonies. Olof Ohman called the tree an "Asp," for Aspen. Black Elk simply uses the term, "cottonwood tree," and in common usage those tree names are often interchanged. One dictionary definition of aspen is "any of the various species of poplar," and secondarily "with leaves that tremble in the slightest breeze," and in the same dictionary cottonwood is defined as, "any of the several American species of poplar." While the Dakotas preferred a true aspen, if none were available, then it seems a cottonwood was acceptable. When an aspen or cottonwood tree is cut down and placed again in the earth, the tree may take root, and continue to grow. If some root should be left with the tree, the chances for regeneration are increased, or the root itself may send up new growing sprouts. When a cottonwood tree is cut down, the roots left in the ground will send up new sprouts and one or more of these will develop into a new tree. I believe that the Dakota's observance of this phenomenon was the source of their prayer for the tree to bloom. Black Elk says "the tree which was selected to be at the center of your sacred hoop is this. May it always flourish and bloom in a *wakan* manner" (Brown 1953: 29).

The Dakota Indians may have buried the KRS, either as part of a ritual ceremony, or as their method of abandonment. Even if their purpose was abandonment, it is very likely that the KRS was buried with some ceremony or ritual. Therefore one must look to Dakota tradition for instances where their ceremonies include large or important stones, where a hole is dug and the stone is placed therein. The best source for a description of several of such Dakota rites probably is *The Sacred Pipe. Black Elk's Account of the Seven Rites of the Oglala Sioux* (1953). Most accounts describing Dakota Indian rites vary in detail, which means that we should understand that Black Elk was recounting tradition and not reciting detailed rules from a text. It is also likely the rites described by Black Elk have undergone changes. His description may have varied considerably from an account given by his ancestors. However, a central idea that is common to several rites is the Dakota practice of burying a stone that represents spiritual power. For example, in Black Elk's account of *Inipi*, the rite of purification he explains that ". . . this first rock is for Wakan-Tanka, who is always at the center of everything " (Brown 1953: 36). In the crying for a vision ritual he says that the first rock, "now very hot, is placed at the center of the sacred hole" (Brown 1953: 52). After the hole has been filled, Black Elk described chants that were then offered, as follows: "O ancient rocks, *Tunkayatakapaka*, you are now here with us; *Wakan-Tanka* has made the Earth . . ." (Brown 1953: 37). Later in the ceremony these words are called out: "O Grandfather

Wakan-Tanka, You are above everything! It is You who have placed a sacred rock upon the earth, which is now at the center of our hoop" (Brown 1953: 39). As the Dakota rite continues, similar statements are chanted, including: "O rocks who are helping us here, listen" (Brown 1953: 56). And: "O you ancient rocks who are sacred, you have neither ears nor eyes, yet you hear and see all things" (Brown 1953: 56). It is not difficult to see a similarity in those Dakota rites and the chanting of Christian Ritual. In my opinion, the origin of the Dakota concept that God, their Wakan-Tanka, placed a sacred rock upon the earth, evolved from their interpretation and memory of the monastic prayers used to dedicate the KRS in the fourteenth century.

In the Dakota Sun Dance ritual a great deal of attention is given to selecting an appropriate tree to be erected. It must be of the cottonwood family, preferably an aspen. In the Sun Dance the Dakotas place their sacred tree in the hole, on or near the sacred stone, and then fill it so the tree will stand upright. It is very clear just what kind of tree it must be. Black Elk says: ". . . one of the standing peoples has been chosen to be at our center; he is the *wagachun* (the rustling tree, or cottonwood)" (Brown 1953: 69). The procuring of the tree was important, and Black Elk says: ". . . it was necessary to locate the sacred rustling tree which was to stand at the center of the Sun Dance . . ." (Brown 1953: 73). Black Elk said: ". . . you O rustling cottonwood have been chosen in a sacred manner, you are about to go to the center of the people's sacred hoop" (Brown 1953: 74). One reason why the aspen was the preferred type of cottonwood tree was explained by Black Elk: ". . . even in the very lightest breeze you can hear the voice of the cottonwood tree; this we understand is its prayer to the Great Spirit" (Brown 1953: 75).

Jonathan Carver and the
Kensington Rune Stone

J
ONATHAN CARVER EXPLORED PARTS OF THE INTE-
rior of North America during 1766–68. From November 14,
1766 until May 1, 1767, he lived with the Dakota Indians who
were then living along the Mississippi River, where St. Paul,
Minnesota is now located. He recorded his experiences in a journal published as a book in 1778. The Dakotas who Carver contacted had only moved to the Mississippi River area a few years
earlier, after they had been driven from the Mille Lacs area by the
Ojibway Indians. Scholars who are familiar with the book of his
travels will be surprised to learn that an entry in Carver's journal,
that was not included in his book, suggests that when he first saw
the cave that became known as Carver's Cave, he also saw the
Kensington Rune Stone.

Carver is best remembered in Minnesota for locating that
cave in the soft sandstone rock that underlies the high bluffs
along the Mississippi River in St. Paul. The cave was an attraction
well-known during the early years of settlement but has since
been demolished or closed off by construction. In his book,
Carver described the cave and also described carvings he saw on
the walls of the cave, to-wit: "I found in this cave many Indian
hieroglyphicks, which appeared very ancient, for time had nearly
covered them with moss, so that it was with difficulty I could
trace them. They were cut in a rude manner upon the inside of the
walls, which were composed of a stone so extremely soft that it

Jonathan Carver.
This 1780 portrait of
the explorer appeared
in an early edition of
his travels.
Photograph courtesy
of Minnesota His-
torical Society.

might easily be
penetrated with a
knife; a stone every
where to be found near
the Mississippi" (Carver
1784: 40). Because the layer of
soft sandstone in the lower face of the bluffs along the Mississippi
is easily carved, Carver's report of seeing what he called "hieroglyphicks" on the walls of the cave would not be likely to have any
relationship to the KRS. Since that is the only reference to stone
carvings included in his book, Carver appeared to have nothing
to tell us about the KRS.

Professor John Parker of Minneapolis became interested in
Carver's adventure, and in the course of his study, examined
Carver's original journal located in the British Museum, from
which the book of his travels had been prepared. The original
journal had never been published until Parker included it in his
book on Carver published in 1976. Comparing the original journal with the published book reveals that Carver recorded another
observation of hieroglyphics on the same day as his entry about
the cave, however his second observation was not included in the
published book.

The description of the cave in the book closely follows the
journal language. The next entry varies considerably. The published book version was: "At a little distance from this dreary cav-

ern is the burying place of several bands of the Naudowessie (Dakota) Indians; though these people have no fixed residence, living in tents, and abiding but a few months on one spot, yet they always bring the bones of their dead to this place; which they take the opportunity of doing when the chiefs meet to hold their councils, and to settle all public affairs for the ensuing summer" (Carver 1784: 40). Carver's Journal entry was:

> Near this cave is the burying place of the Mottobauntoway band of the Naudowessee. A few months before I came here dyed and was buryed the chief of this band. I went to see the grave. It is impossible for me to describe all the hieroglyphicks and significant marks of regard and distinction this people had paid to the memory of this deceased grandee, much more then I had ever seen of the kind among any nations I had passed before (Parker 1976: 92).

There is nothing in Dakota history, archeologically or traditionally, that would explain what Carver described as "hieroglyphicks" on the grave of an important chief. It is my belief that Carver had been shown the KRS, and because he knew nothing of Scandinavian runes he wrote that they looked like "hieroglyphicks." The shape of the KRS resembles a tombstone. When Carver saw it he probably assumed that it was a tombstone in honor of a chief, and his assumption was the basis for his entry in his journal.

Probably the reason why he omitted that second reference to "hieroglyphicks" from his book is because during his long stay with the Dakotas, he learned that he had been in error in his assumption that the hieroglyphics he had described in his journal marked a chief's grave. During his visit he learned about Dakota burial customs, which he described in his book and substituted for the journal entry. While Carver was able to get better information about Dakota burial practice, he probably was never able to learn any more from the Dakotas about the "hieroglyphicks" that he had seen at the burial ground, that he had described in his journal, and so he omitted that report.

According to Professor Raymond J. DeMallie, who evaluated and edited Carver's efforts at compiling a Dakota dictionary, which was also published in Parker's book, Carver must have relied on a type of "pidgin" Dakota (Parker 1976: 212). That language barrier would indicate that whatever the Dakotas may have tried to explain about the significance of the "hieroglyphicks" that Carver saw at the burial ground would have been beyond his comprehension.

I believe that when the Dakotas left Mille Lacs, in about 1750, they took the KRS with them, which would mean that the Dakotas who Carver contacted in 1766 had it in their possession. Because the Dakotas knew from their history that the KRS came into being during a visitation by white men, they probably thought that Carver would appreciate seeing it. On the day he arrived one of the first things they did was to take him to the place where the stone was kept. To Carver, the KRS would certainly have looked like a tombstone, which he wrote in his journal entry. Accounts of early Dakota Indian life do not relate any Dakota Indian custom of marking graves with tombstones covered with carved figures or hieroglyphics. Further Dakota history does not suggest that they usually brought visitors to their burial sites.

The likely location of the Dakota burial ground was in what is now called Indian Mounds Park (Parker 1976: 93). That site is on the top of the bluffs along the Mississippi and has no soft sandstone rock formations. Archaeological study indicates that the Dakotas had discontinued the practice of building burial mounds in about the 14th century, although they continued to use numerous old mounds, like those in the Indian Mounds Park site, for intrusive burials of bones that they collected from scaffold burials. Because the Dakota understood that the KRS involved death and was an object of great mystery and power, the Indian Mounds Park site would have been a logical place for them to keep the KRS, where they probably kept it covered by buffalo hides to

INDIAN MOUNDS, ST. PAUL, MINN.

Indian Mounds Park, St. Paul, Minnesota, circa 1910.
View of the park at the top of the bluff, overlooking the Mississippi River,
where the Dakotas may have shown the KRS to Jonathan Carver.
Photographic postcard from the author's collection.

limit its power. Later, when the Dakotas moved west to sites
along the Minnesota River, they carried the KRS with them.

Because the KRS resembles a tombstone, and because the
Dakota probably approached it with respect, it would have been
reasonable for Carver to arrive at a first impression that it was a
Dakota tombstone, and because of the many carved figures on it,
to assume that it was one obviously made for an important leader.
Under those circumstances it also would have been natural for
Carver to adopt a respectful and reverent posture when he viewed
the stone. His show of respect towards the KRS may have been
interpreted by the Dakotas to mean that Carver was able to understand the meaning of the runes carved in the stone; and if so,
his perceived ability to do so may have caused them to think that
Carver had some connection to its mystical power. That would
indicate to the Dakotas that Carver's visit was related to their legendary past. The Dakota Indians had probably seen each of their
earlier white contacts as possible links to that ancient visitation,

and by happenstance, Carver's actions when viewing the KRS may have confirmed their hopes in his case. That may explain why he seems to have been unusually warmly welcomed by the Dakotas.

While my analysis of Carver's Journal is not proof that he saw the KRS; the fact remains that Carver's journal entry describing hieroglyphics exists, and his use of the term "hieroglyphics" clearly implies that the marks he saw were carved in stone. There was no Dakota tradition of carving stone tombstones such as Carver described in his Journal; and so it is difficult to find any other explanation for Carver's journal entry about the hieroglyphic markings, other than as, in fact, his description of the KRS.

Lone Dog's Winter Count

WINTER COUNT IS THE NAME GIVEN TO DAKOTA Indian pictorial records showing the history of their tribe. This is because the Dakotas marked the passage of a year by reference to the winter. At least sixty of these winter counts are known (Howard 1979: 5). The most famous, and most copied, is Lone Dog's Winter Count, which was featured in a double page color print in the *Fourth Annual Report of the Bureau of American Ethnology for 1882–1883* and again in the *Tenth Annual Report of the U.S. Bureau of American Ethnology for 1888–1889*. In both instances it was used to illustrate long articles by Col. Garrick Mallery concerning Indian picture writing. The print shows Lone Dog's Winter Count as it was first known, copied on cloth. The count begins in the center of the hide on the right, reads to the left and then spirals outward. In his 1886 study Mallery compared Lone Dog's Winter Count with several others and found that the first five pictures in Lone Dog's Winter Count were also present in nearly identical form in the others (Mallery 1886: 103). That similarity suggests that each was copied from an earlier work showing traditional history, and was not the firsthand observation of an annual event by the artist who prepared the count.

Battiste Good's Winter Count is in a far different style and shows Dakota traditional history in a series of circles, supposedly beginning with the year 901 and ending in 1700, when the more conventional style of annual events begins, and runs through 1880 (Mallery 1893: 288).

The winter counts generally lack interpretive language. However, it seems clear that, in most cases, the counts use two approaches to Dakota history. The first group of five pictures relates to Dakota traditional history, while the second and much larger portion of the counts shows an event from each successive year that was seen as the most significant by the artist.

In Lone Dog's Winter Count the beginning pictures appear to include the tradition of the White Buffalo Woman, the acquisition of horses and the Sacred Pipe. What has not been clear is the significance of the Count's first picture, which is in the shape of a vertical rectangle covered with vertical lines. It was probably copied from earlier counts and its story had become lost. That leaves the question: what other aspect of Dakota Indian history was significant enough to rank ahead of all others, so that it was the subject of the first picture? In my opinion the answer is that the first picture was intended to show the stone that Dakota Indian Spiritual Tradition identifies as the first step in the creation of the world, the stone they call their Grandfather; and the artist who created that concept of what their "Grandfather" looked like used the KRS for his model

In the 1880's, Mallery apparently had not considered the possibility that the pictures of Lone Dog's Winter Count did not relate to annual events, and in the case of the first picture he gave its meaning as follows:

> Thirty Dakotas were killed by Crow Indians. The device consists of thirty parallel black lines in three columns, the outer lines being united. In this chart, such black lines always signify the death of Dakotas killed by their enemies (Mallery 1886: 103).

The informants whom Mallery relied upon for his interpretation were apparently mistaken, unwilling, or unable to tell him

Lone Dog's Winter Count.
In the 1870's both Garrick Mallery and Col. Richard Dodge collected copies on cloth of the Winter Count kept by Lone Dog, a Yanktonai Sioux. The count begins in the center.
Lithograph from Garrick Mallery, "Pictographs of the North American Indians," (1886).

the true meaning. Mallery did comment on the seemingly mundane beginning picture in Lone Dog's winter count, writing:

> The earliest character (the one in the center or beginning of the spiral) merely represents the killing of a small number of Dakotas by their enemies, an event of frequent occurrence, and neither so important nor interesting as many others of the seventy-one shown in the chart, more than one of which, indeed, might well have been selected as a notable fixed point before and after which simple arithmetical notation could have been used to mark the years (Mallery 1886: 92).

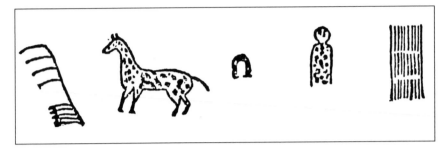

The first five pictures in Lone Dog's Winter Count, beginning on the right. Adopted from lithograph of Garrick Mallery, "Pictographs of the North American Indians," (1886).

While the true meaning of the first picture may have been unknown by the Dakotas who Mallery consulted, nevertheless the interpretation they gave him, and the picture itself, reveal several aspects that I believe point directly to the KRS.

The most obvious is that the shape, a vertical rectangle, is in about the same shape and proportion as the KRS. If the first picture was intended to be a representation of the first stone of creation, the Dakota's Grandfather and the genesis of creation, then the shape of that stone, drawn by the original artist is significant. The shape of the first picture is not common to other objects in the Dakota world. Recalling and reproducing the shape of an object is basic when telling a story with pictures, so the shape of an object would be the most likely aspect or detail to be remembered. That the first picture and the KRS are similarly shaped is more than somewhat coincidental. A stone may be round, or irregular but the first picture shows a remarkably geometric shape of the same proportions as the KRS.

It is my hypothesis that the Dakota Indian belief that the world began with a stone, is a concept that evolved from their limited understanding of the teachings that they received from the monks who carved the KRS in the 14th century. This they then combined with their ideas of mystery that they attributed to the KRS itself. Their concept may have also been reinforced by their rudimentary understanding of the Genesis account of creation, and after learning that the Ten Commandments were carved on stone. Add to those ideas the Dakotas' mistaken notion that when one reads aloud from an inscription carved in stone, that it was the stone speaking, and you have a plausible explanation for how the Dakota Indians came to believe that stones were the first step in the creation of the world. To understand how that could have happened we must appreciate the whole circumstance of the KRS from the Dakotas' perspective. It was carved by remarkable visitors—who possessed great skill and knowledge, and who were large strong men armed with iron weapons. Yet, these visitors were peaceful, sought to be helpful and wanted to share their wisdom. The Dakotas believed that their visitors were sharing the secrets of their power with them. That notion was reinforced since their European visitors also believed that to be true. Thus, the first Dakota artist who sought to create an image to represent the beginning of the world chose to draw the shape of the stone that represented that beginning in the shape of the KRS, probably based on his firsthand observation of the KRS.

The second aspect of the first picture that relates to the KRS is its representation of the number, "thirty," according to Mallery's interpretation. Thirty is also the number of individuals (8 Goths and 22 Norrmen) who are described in the KRS inscription as comprising the exploring party. The Dakotas could not read the inscription, but they could count, and the number of men represented in the first picture, according to Mallery's interpretation, is the same number as reported in the KRS inscription. If that is a coincidence, it certainly is unusual. In my view it is another reason to conclude that the KRS was the original inspiration for the first picture.

The third common aspect is that the first picture, according to Mallery, tells of deaths, as does the KRS. We can assume that the 14th century Dakota Indians knew of the deaths of the ten explorers; and we can assume that when the KRS inscription was carved that the explorers told their Dakota hosts that the inscription told of those deaths. One might ask, why should vertical marks in the first picture be a sign of death? The answer probably is that there is no reason, other than, as described below, the original artist used vertical markings to simulate a text. Because the Dakotas knew that the KRS told of death, they applied that meaning to the vertical marks that the artist used in drawing the picture.

The fourth aspect is that the first picture has extensive markings in vertical lines that mimic the look of the carved runic text, such as seen in the KRS inscription. Often a drawing is only an outline of an object, while in the first picture the whole surface is covered with marks that suggests that the artist who first drew the picture, perhaps many years before, was aware that the KRS had extensive carvings cut into its surface. The artist was able to simulate that look with vertical markings, and in addition, by using thirty of such marks, he also communicated the information that there were thirty explorers.

It is ironic that the publication of Lone Dog's Winter Count, including its representation of the KRS, in the 1880s, preceded the discovery of the KRS by over a decade; and that a century would pass after its discovery before the similarity of its first picture and the KRS would be recognized.

The first picture of Battiste Good's Winter Count shows a white buffalo calf and a pipe and is interpreted to tell of the appearance of the Woman from Heaven and her gift of the Sacred Pipe to the Dakotas. It seems clear from this picture that the Dakotas begin their history as a people from the teachings of the White Buffalo Woman, a legend which I believe grew from the picture of the Virgin Mary and the teachings attributed to her by the explorers who carved the KRS.

→ Part III ←

The Ojibway

The Ojibway Emergence

THE STORY OF THE OJIBWAY DOES NOT INCLUDE
the carving of the KRS inscription, but it does relate, I
believe, to events that occurred subsequently. Their story
is relevant because it suggests what happened next to the explorers who carved the KRS after they left the Mille Lacs region, and
explains their role in creating the Ojibway culture. Specifically, it
also includes the amazing story of the Mundua people who, I believe, were Europeans living in the St. Lawrence, who were par-
ticipants in the expedition of Europeans who carved the KRS,
and who became the Marten Totem or clan of the Ojibway. They
eventually led the Ojibway to the western end of Lake Superior,
and then to the Mille Lacs region in Minnesota, where their descendants live today in a community named Vineland.

Earlier I have asserted that the monks whom I believe carved
the KRS, came from a monastic community that had established
itself near the settlements of the immigrants from Greenland, in
the western St. Lawrence Gulf area, several years prior to 1362.
Helge Ingstad, and others, have concluded that the Norse who
abandoned their Western Settlement in Greenland in 1347 then
moved to Vinland (Ingstad 1966: 324). If so, then they probably
had contact with the proto-Ojibway Indians. It may be that
European monks, and possibly other Europeans, followed the
Greenland settlers into the St. Lawrence region.

It is also my thought that the exploring party that went west consisted of 40 men, led by monks who were Goths and their European servants, with the balance of the party being made up of Norse who were former Greenland residents, and two Indians, who guided the group. Probably the guides had previously traveled west to explore and to trade, and knew the route. Possibly it was intriguing stories about the west, told by the guides, that aroused the curiosity of the monks and so prompted the exploration.

I believe that in 1363, the European explorers who had carved the KRS, left their encampment at Knife Lake, which was located one day's journey south of Lake Mille Lacs, retraced their route to where their ships had been left in the care of ten men, and sailed east on Lake Superior, to return to the St. Lawrence, and Vinland.

While on their return, possibly one of their party died, and was buried along with medieval Norse weapons on the north shore of Lake Superior, creating what has been called the Beardmore find. If the explorers followed the north shore of Lake Superior on their return east, the Beardmore site would have been along their route. Historian Farley Mowat has suggested a possible relationship between the Beardmore find and the KRS. He also pointed out that Johannes Brondsted, a Danish authority on antiquities, examined both the Beardmore artifacts and the KRS, and saw no reason to doubt their authenticity (Mowat 1965: 301).

When the explorers reached the St. Lawrence they found a state of near collapse because of the Black Death, which had killed Europeans and Indians alike. To improve their mutual chance of survival, various local Indians, the remaining Europeans, and the returning explorers joined together. They developed a system to identify each of the various groups that had merged into their new tribe by giving each a totem or clan name, using the names of animals or birds. The Europeans, consisting of those who had returned from the west and the surviving Europeans remaining along the St. Lawrence, mainly women and children, took the totemic or clan designation of Marten, which is a small fur bearing animal.

This new tribe, I believe, is the same tribe that William W.

Warren chose to call the Ojibway, and is the group whose history he traces back to the 14th century to a time when they lived on salt water, presumably near the mouth of the St. Lawrence River (Warren 1885: 76). They now live in many separate groups, favoring various names, including Ojibway and Chippewa. I have used the name Ojibway, following the usage adopted by Warren in his book, *History of the Ojibway*, written in about 1850-1. Warren's work focuses on the Ojibway who expanded west from their settlement at Sault Ste. Marie, to the south shore of Lake Superior, and into Wisconsin and Minnesota. Those Ojibway include the members of the Marten Totem. The Ojibway of the Marten Totem differ in their appearance, having European features, and I believe that they were the source of the major European influences that scholars have observed in Ojibway culture.

Ronald J. Mason, author of *Great Lakes Archaeology*, reports no archaeological evidence that the Ojibway Indians existed as a tribal unit until the coming of the Europeans (Mason 1981: 9). Presumably that judgment was based on the fact that the earliest known Ojibway sites also contained European objects, and the assumption that they must have been of post-Columbian origin. I contend that such European objects may have been the result of pre-Columbian contact, so that the mere presence of a European object does not conclusively prove it to be of post-Columbian origin. Mason also postulates that several small Indian groups joined together, after a major outbreak of disease, to become the Ojibway, and that the Totem (clan) designations within the Ojibway Nation refer back to those original smaller groups (Mason 1981: 9). I agree. However, I contend that the disaster that caused the small groups to merge was the Black Death of the 14th century.

A 1998 study at the Center for Molecular Medicine at Emory University Medical School showed that Ojibway Indians in the Great Lakes region carry Mitochondrial DNA markers revealing significant European pre-Columbian contact through the maternal line. "For the Native Americans, this haplogroup encompasses approximately 25% of the Ojibway" (Wallace 1998: 7). These DNA findings certainly offer support to show why European aspects of Ojibway Culture are evidence of pre-Columbian contact.

Warren puts the earliest history of the Ojibway in the 14th century, contemporaneous with the KRS inscription and the Black Death. Soon thereafter they began their migration west (Warren 1885: 79). Evidence of Ojibway settlement further west has been found near the present city of Peterborough, Ontario, where extensive petroglyphs carved in stone dated to before 1400 were discovered in 1954. Subsequently the Ojibway divided and one group established a large community at the outlet of Lake Superior, at Sault Ste. Marie. Later, in about 1490, they continued their expansion west to establish a community at La Pointe, located on Madeline Island in the Apostle Islands of Lake Superior, near its south shore (Warren 1885: 90). The Ojibway continued to expand along the south shore of Lake Superior, and probably by about 1700 had reached the western end of Lake Superior where they founded a settlement named Fond du Lac, located just west of present-day Duluth, Minnesota, where they continue to reside today. The Ojibway settlement at Fond du Lac was founded by a member of the Marten clan named Wamegisugo. The chiefs of the Fond du Lac settlement, when Warren wrote his history, were that founder's direct descendants (Warren 1885: 84, 129).

Thanks to the portrait of a Fond du Lac Chief named Ongewae, a member of the Marten Clan, painted by Charles Bird King in 1827, we have an example of the appearance that may have been characteristic of the men of the Marten Clan that Warren mentioned (Warren 1885: 94). Ongewae looks to be of European extraction and has curly hair. The portrait was published in a lithograph by McKenney and Hall. An illustration of their 1834 print is included in this book. We know that Ongewae was a member of the Marten Clan because a picture of a Marten was included in his portrait.

In the field of ethnohistory a major issue is whether or not aspects of a culture were acquired from outside sources, or evolved internally within the group. Often the answer to that question turns on the nature of the subject, and on what is known about the exposure to outsiders. If no outside contact is known, then the assumption may be made that the culture must have developed internally. If it is clear that the nature of the subject is such that some outside contact must have been required, then the issue becomes one of discovering that contact. These ethnohistory issues have been debated among scholars in respect to the culture of the Ojibway for over 150 years. I believe that our new understanding of the KRS should now settle many of those longstanding debates about the source of the outside cultural influences that have been observed in the Ojibway culture for so long.

The evidence of Judeo-Christian influence appeared so obvious to scholars in the 19th century that one widely held view was that the Ojibway were descended from one of the ten lost tribes of Israel (Warren 1885: 62). Those 19th century writers were close enough to the Ojibway in their native state to appreciate that post-Columbian missionary activity could not have been the source of their culture, and so they turned to the lost tribe of Israel idea as the most likely explanation.

The lost tribe of Israel thesis no longer has any advocates

Ongewae, an Ojibway man of the Marten clan. Charles Bird King painted this portrait of the Ojibway leader in 1827. The painting was published as a lithograph in McKenney and Hall, *Indian Tribes of North America* (1836–1843). Collection of the author.

because scholars have determined that there were no lost tribes of Israel and even if there were, world geography would make such a migration impossible. Today scholars tend to ignore the issue, or, being many generations removed from the native culture, now feel safe to suggest that Ojibway culture, to the extent that it shows European influence, must be attributed to their quick study of post-Columbian missionary teaching.

While the Judeo-Christian influence was obvious to early scholars, it must have been appreciated that the Norse contact described in the sagas of circa 1000 A.D. could not have been the source because the time of those voyages predated significant establishment of Norse Christianity. The historians and anthropologists who wrote of the North American Indians had little knowledge of medieval European history, particularly of 14th century Scandinavia, and northern European Protestant historians were generally uninterested in the Roman Catholic Church era of their history. So the presence of the Church, represented by monks, in North America in the 14th century was not considered.

Wub-e-ke-niew, a Minnesota Ojibway Indian, considered the issue recently and concluded that the Ojibway of whom William Warren wrote, and Warren himself, were "white Indians" (Wub-e-ke-niew 1995: 76). He saw the Ojibway or Chippewa culture as described by Warren and others as European, not Indian. He attributes those European aspects to the influence of post-Columbian missionaries, presumably because it seemed to be the only explanation. While Wub-e-ke-niew is on sound ground in describing Warren's Ojibway as "white Indians," he is wrong about the reason. For example, in his 1991 history, Peter S. Schmalz wrote, "Early missionaries in the Great Lakes region found the Ojibway religion strong and resistant to change... It was not until the mid-nineteenth century that Christianity made any serious impression on the Ojibway" (Schmalz 1991: 10). Warren clearly never considered post-Columbian influence to be a factor. He wrote:

The analogies which have been noticed as existing between the Hebrew and Algic tribes have not struck my attention individually: others whom I have consulted, living as isolated among the Ojibway as I have been, holding daily communion with them, speaking their language, hearing their legends and lodge stories, and withal, readers of the Bible, have fallen into the same belief, and this simple fact is itself full worthy of notice (Warren 1885: 75).

It is my opinion that the Biblical and Christian influence that Warren and many others observed in the Ojibway culture was very extensive and was known by them in great detail, indicating that it had deep well-established old roots. Those circumstances point much more likely to a source earlier than post-Columbian missionary activity. In the following pages I will present a more detailed study of particular aspects of that culture, which supports the proposition that this influence was in fact the outgrowth of 14th century European contact.

The Totem or Clan System

T HE OJIBWAY WERE COMPRISED OF A NUMBER OF smaller, clan-like groups of families called totems. Totem was the correct and traditional name for these groups, however modern usage has connected the term "totem" with West Coast Indians and totem poles. Therefore to avoid confusion I will use the word "clan" for totem when describing the Ojibway system. Warren listed 21 different Ojibway clans. He states, however, that in the 1850s eight-tenths of the Ojibway belonged to the six largest clans, which were the crane, catfish, bear, marten, wolf and loon (Warren 1885: 45). Initially the system may have referred back to the specific smaller groups of Indians who had merged to become the Ojibway. I believe that the reason why the clan system continued and grew stronger was because of the strong influence of the European Ojibway who were concerned about obeying Roman Catholic Church law prohibiting marriage between closely related individuals. That Church law was enforced by the clan rule that a man could not marry a female who was a member of his clan. The result was that a male always retained his clan identity while females became members of their husband's clan.

If the totemic or clan system's purpose had been to perpetuate the identity of a smaller group within the tribe, then one would expect the opposite rule, one where marriage within the clan was required in order to keep the blood line of the clan pure. The only sound reason for the clan rule limiting marriage to those outside the clan was to avoid marriage between closely related individuals. There is scant evidence showing that the aborigines of North America were particularly interested in the degree of consanguinity of marriage partners. However, it was a subject of major interest to the medieval Roman Catholic Church. The Church did not adopt marriage as a sacrament until 1215, and at the same time the Church ruled that marriage was then prohibited within the third degree of consanguinity (Cantor 1993: 418). The degree of consanguinity had become an issue in the Church in the medieval period, but it was not an Indian issue. While the clan rule did not mirror the Church law precisely, it had about the same effect and was easy to apply.

Another reason for the rule may have been to create a system where each male in a clan continued to be a direct descendant of the clan's founders, to cling to some degree of their European identity in the future. The Mundua's choice of the marten instead of a larger animal as their symbol reflects their European values, because the marten is the source of the fur known as American Sable, and sable was then the fur of the nobility in Europe.

It is also clear that the clan system was pre-Columbian. Warren observed that the clan rule limiting marriage to those outside the clan was less observed as the Ojibway were exposed to European contact. Warren described the clan system as "ancient" and wrote that a man marrying someone from his own clan would be like a white man marrying his sister (Warren 1885: 42).

The Mundua Story

WARREN'S *HISTORY OF THE OJIBWAY* INCLUDES the story of the Mundua people whom we first meet living on the shore of the St. Lawrence Gulf. The Mundua were described by Indians as noticeably different people who kept to themselves. The Indian description of the Mundua seemed to describe Europeans. My opinion is that the Mundua legend, as recounted by Warren, was the 19th century Ojibway account of the incorporation of the survivors of the Scandinavian settlements that once existed in the St. Lawrence region into the local Indian community after those settlements had been decimated by the plague. Warren wrote:

> One tradition, however, is deemed full worthy of notice, and while offering it as an historical fact, it will at the same time answer as a specimen of the mythological character of their tales which reach as far back as this period.

> During their residence in the East, the Ojibway have a distinct tradition of having annihilated a tribe whom they denominate Mun-dua. Their old men, whom I have questioned on this subject, do not all agree in the location or details. Their disagreements, however, are not very material, and I will proceed to give, verbatim, the version of Kah-nin-dum-a-win-so, the old chief of Sandy Lake:

'There was at one time living on the shores of a great lake, a numerous and powerful tribe of people; they lived congregated in one single town, which was so large that a person standing on a hill which stood in its centre, could not see the limits of it. This tribe, whose name was Mun-dua, were fierce and warlike; their hand was against every other tribe, and the captives whom they took in war were burned with fire as offerings to their spirits.

'All the surrounding tribes lived in great fear of them, till their Ojibway brothers called them to council and sent the wampum and war club, to collect the warriors of all the tribes with whom they were related. A war party was thus raised, whose line of warriors reached, as they marched in single file, as far as the eye could see. They proceeded against the great town of their common enemy, to put out their fire forever. They surrounded and attacked them from all quarters where their town was not bounded by the lake shore, and though overwhelming in their numbers, yet the Mun-dua had such confidence in their own force and prowess, that on the first day, they sent only their boys to repel the attack. The boys being defeated and driven back, on the second day the young men turned out to beat back their assailants. Still the Ojibway and their allies stood their ground and gradually drove them in, till on the eve of the second day, they found themselves in possession of half the great town. The Mun-duas now became awake to their danger, and on the third day, beginning to consider it a serious business, their old and tried warriors, 'mighty men of valor' sang their war songs, and putting on their paints and ornaments of battle, they turned out to repel their invaders.

'The fight this day was hand to hand. There is nothing in their traditional accounts, to equal the fierceness of the struggle described in this battle. The bravest men, probably, in America, had met—one party fighting for vengeance, glory, and renown; and the other for everything dear to man, home, family, for very existence itself!

'The Mun-dua were obliged at last to give way, and hotly pressed by their foes, women and children threw themselves into, and perished in the lake. At this juncture their aged chief, who had witnessed the unavailing defence of his people, and who saw the ground covered with the bodies of his greatest warriors, called with a loud voice on the 'Great Spirit' for help (for besides being Chief of the Munduas, he was also a great medicine man and juggler).

'Being a wicked people, the Great Spirit did not listen to the prayer of their chief for deliverance. The aged medicine man then called upon the spirits of the water and of the earth, who are the under spirits of the 'Great Spirit of Evil,' and immediately a dark and heavy fog arose from the bosom of the lake, and covered in folds of darkness the site of the vanquished town, and the scene of the bloody battle. The old chieftain by his voice gathered together the remnants of his slaughtered tribe, and under cover of the Evil Spirit's fog, they left their homes forever. The whole day and ensuing night they traveled to escape from their enemies, until a gale of wind, which the medicine men of the Ojibway had asked the Great Spirit to raise, drove away the fog; the surprise of the fleeing Mun-duas was extreme when they found themselves standing on a hill back of their deserted town, and in plain view of their enemies.

'It is the will of the Great Spirit that we should perish,' exclaimed their old chief; but once more they dragged their wearied limbs in hopeless flight. They ran into an adjacent forest where they buried the women and children in the ground, leaving but a small aperture to enable them to breathe. The men then turned back, and once more they met their pursuing foes in a last mortal combat. They

fought stoutly for a while, when again overpowered by
numbers, they turned and fled, but in a different direction
from the spot where they had secreted their families; but a
few men escaped, who afterward returned, and disinterred
the women and children. This small remnant of a once
powerful tribe were the next year attacked by an Ojibway
war-party, taken captive, and incorporated in this tribe.
Individuals are pointed out to this day who are of Mun-dua
descent, and who are members of the respected family
whose totem is the Marten (Warren 1885: 91-94).

Earlier in his book, Warren described the Totems, or clans, of the
Ojibway, and wrote this about the Marten Totem:

The Waub-ish-a-she, or Marten family, form a numerous
body in the tribe, and is one of the leading clans. Tradition
says that they are sprung from the remnant captives of a
fierce and warlike tribe whom the coalesced Algic tribes
have exterminated, and whom they denominate the Mundua. The chiefs Waub-ish-ash (the Marten), of Chippe-
way River, Shin-goob (Balsam), and Nug-aun-ub (Sitting-
ahead), of Fond du Lac, are now the principal men of the
clan. The celebrated Ke-che-waub-ish-ash, of Sandy Lake,
Sha-wa-ke-shig, of Leech Lake, and Muk-ud-a-shib (or
Black Duck), of Red River, were members of this family. In
their days they conduced greatly towards wresting country
from the Dakotas, and driving them westward. All three
died on battlefields ... (Warren 1885: 50).

Warren's observation that, "individuals are pointed out to this
day who are of Mun-dua descent," confirms that the Mun-dua
were not mythical and had a distinctive appearance. Warren did
not explain how such individuals could be identified, but there is
the 1827 portrait of chief Ongewae, a member of the Marten Totem
from Fond du Lac, that reveals European features, particularly his
curly hair, which is a common Scandinavian characteristic.

The Mundua story also includes a detail that probably is a specific reference to the return of the party of explorers who created the KRS. That reference was to "a few men escaped who afterward returned and . . . were the next year attacked by the Ojibway war-party, taken captive, and incorporated in this tribe." The idea of a battle such as the story supposes, lasting over a winter and resuming the next year, is completely unlike usual Indian conflicts. The interpretation of that reference in the Mundua story probably should be that many of the men of the Mundua settlements were away on a trip exploring the west when their home settlements collapsed, and when the men returned the next year, they, along with their surviving women and children were adopted into the Ojibway community and became the Marten Totem.

Telling history in terms of battle is a common Indian way of telling stories to make them more interesting, and perhaps to put them in a context that 19th century Indians could relate to. If one considers Warren's Mundua battle account literally, we are told that the massive Indian attack by a line of warriors so long to be "as far as the eye could see," was stopped by only young boys for two days, while the strong defenders ignored the fight. The three days probably indicates that there were three separate European settlements, located fairly close together, and that while these settlements were being decimated by the plague, curious nearby Indians wandered in to see what was happening. We know from European reports of the Black Death that adult males were the most common victims of the disease, and also if many of the men from the European settlements were off on a trip exploring the west, then we can understand why the Indians perceived that only children, youth and old men were available to defend the settlements. The plague may have left many dead and unburied, and there may well have been evidence of profuse bleeding at death, all of which could have suggested to the curious Indians that a major battle had been waged. As the Marten Totem became a large and important part of the Ojibway world, it seems clear that the Mundua were not "exterminated," as the legend claims. After being exposed to the plague, it was the Indians' turn to suffer the consequences. When the explorers returned from the west the next summer, the Indian population had also been severely reduced. Under those circumstances the only reasonable choice for the returning explorers was to join the group to protect and care for the European women and children, adding their numbers to the group so it could better sustain and protect itself. Shortly thereafter this newly constituted Ojibway Nation sought greater safety by moving west.

The Midewiwin or Grand Medicine Society

P
ROBABLY THE BEST EVIDENCE THAT THE LAKE
Superior Ojibway Indians were deeply involved in pre-
Columbian European contact is their institution known as
the Midewiwin or Grand Medicine Society, which was their dominant cultural institution. The Midewiwin Society was described in
great detail by W. J. Hoffman in the *Seventh Annual Report of the
Bureau of American Ethnology*. In contrast to some modern scholars
who think the Midewiwin reflects the influence of early post-
Columbian missionaries, Hoffman explained that the strongest
opposition to the introduction of Christianity to the Ojibway
came from the leaders of the Midewiwin Society, writing that:

> ... the cause of this antagonism is seen to lie in the fact that
> the traditions of Indian genesis and cosmogony and the
> ritual of initiation into the Society of the Midé constitute
> what is to them a religion, even more powerful and impres-
> sive than the Christian religion is to the average civilized
> man. This opposition still exists among the leading classes
> of a number of the Algonkian tribes, and especially among
> the Ojibway, many bands of whom have been more or less
> isolated and beyond convenient reach of the Church
> (Hoffman 1891: 151).

Hoffman also commented on the observations of Father Jacques
Marquette, an early missionary who had a brief contact with the

Ojibway in about 1679, at Green Bay on the western shore of Lake Michigan. Marquette had written:

When I arriv'd there, I was very glad to see a great Cross set up in the middle of the Village, adorn'd with several White Skins, Red Girdles, Bows and Arrows, which that good People had offer'd to the Great Manitou, to return him their Thanks for the care he had taken of them during the Winter . . . (Hoffman 1891: 151).

Hoffman commented that:

Marquette was without doubt ignorant of the fact that the cross is the sacred post, and the symbol of the fourth degree of the Midewiwin Society. The erroneous conclusion that the cross was erected as evidence of the adoption of Christianity, and possibly as a compliment to the visitor, was a natural one on the part of the priest, but this same symbol of the Midé Society had probably been erected and bedecked with barbaric emblems and weapons months before anything was known of him (Hoffman 1891: 155).

Hoffman included a colored drawing of the Cross, painted white with red spots, used in the Midewiwin Fourth Degree ceremony (Hoffman 1891: 240). The fourth degree was the Midewiwin highest rank and Hoffman noted that the influence by those who "have received four degrees, is beyond belief" (Hoffman 1891: 274). It is unlikely that post-Columbian churchmen would have introduced a white and red color scheme for the Cross.

There were four degrees of Midewiwin membership, each step being more exclusive, with each advance to a higher degree having a particular ceremony. The nature of the rituals and system of degrees of the Midewiwin bear a remarkable similarity to the rituals and ceremonies of the Masonic Lodge, particularly in the case of the Midewiwin fourth degree, which resembles the third degree of the Masons. A comparison of the two, I believe would show sufficient similarity to justify the conclusion that the Mide-wiwin and the Masons share a common European ancestry.

The Masonic Lodge rituals most likely evolved from the rituals practiced by those engaged in the craft of masonry in the medieval period, many of whom lived within the monastic system. The masonry craft organizations of the medieval period most likely adopted rituals that were similar to those used in the monasteries. The KRS was the work of skilled stone workers. It is well known that many medieval monasteries included stone masons who worked as builders, and it is likely that the stone carvers who carved the KRS were monks or associated laymen. It is my hypothesis that the Midewiwin evolved from the rituals of the stone mason monks who became Ojibway in the 14th century. It is my belief that the Peterborough Petroglyphs (described in another chapter) offer additional and dramatic confirmation of the origin of the Ojibway stone carvers. The stone carving skill eventually became lost, and the Midewiwin society survived to function as a religious and leadership organization in succeeding generations. In that respect the development of the Midewiwin in Ojibway society parallels the evolution of Freemasonry in Europe, as it moved away from a lodge of working craftsmen, into a brotherhood and leadership organization.

While the similarity between the Midewiwin and the Masons seemed obvious to me, the anthropologists who have written about the Ojibway have not made the comparison, perhaps because they were not acquainted with Masonic ritual, or because they hesitated to make that comparison for other reasons. However, Warren did observe that, "Amongst the Ojibway, the secrets of this grand rite are as sacredly kept as the secrets of the Masonic Lodge among the whites" (Warren 1885: 66).

A clerk in the fur trade, George Nelson, wrote an extensive journal of his observations of the Northern Ojibway between 1802 and 1823 (a generation before Warren). Nelson had witnessed a Midewiwin initiation at a southern Ojibway location, and described it as: "A ceremony I shall compare to Free-masonry" (Brown and Brightman 1988: 82).

Warren observed that the society, "incorporated most that is ancient amongst them—songs and traditions that have descended, not orally, but in hieroglyphics, for a least a long line of generations. In this rite is also perpetuated the purest and most ancient idioms of their language, which differs somewhat from that of the common every-day use . . ." (Warren 1885: 67). He also noted that their rites include the great rules of life that bear a strong likeness to the Ten Commandments (Warren 1885: 67). Warren was part Ojibway and lived in close contact with their culture and its elders, and from that vantage point never considered the possibility that the Midewiwin came into existence because of the work of early post-Columbian missionaries.

The origin of the Midewiwin Society has been seen as a mystery. Harold Hickerson, a modern scholar and a pioneer in the field of ethnohistory, considered the question when he framed the issue simply: "The problem is discovering when the *Midewiwin* began, and why." He concluded "that the Midewiwin was post contact" (Hickerson 1970: 51). He based his conclusion on the following factors: the Midewiwin ceremonial use of the Cross, a Christian symbol; the need for candidates for degrees to give payment; the occult or mystical aspects of the ceremonies; and lastly, an organised priesthood. All of these, he concluded, were improbable and unlikely aspects to be found in an aboriginal institution (Hickerson 1970: 54). Each of those improbably and unlikely aspects would apply equally, if not more so, if the Midewiwin was begun by medieval stone masons who became influential leaders of the Ojibway several hundred years before the earliest post-Columbian missionaries reached the St. Lawrence region. Hickerson also wrote that he could locate no reference to the Midewiwin in the earliest Jesuit records. He noted that the Midewiwin was not well known throughout the whole Algonquin region of North America, but was limited to the Ojibway in the Lake Superior and Green Bay regions and that the

Ojibway in those areas had contact with post-contact Europeans before their back-country cousins did. The absence of early Jesuit mention of the Midewiwin does not mean that it did not exist, but merely that the Ojibway, who were the chief Midewiwin practitioners, had moved west from the St. Lawrence region before the Jesuits arrived. They had located at La Pointe in Lake Superior in 1490, before Columbus; and so were far away from the territory first visited by the Jesuits. Further, the Midewiwin was a secret society, and the Ojibway did not wish to share its activities with white men. Hickerson's second and third arguments, that the Midewiwin was mainly an institution of the Ojibway in the Lake Superior area, and was along the main trade route, do suggest European contact, but again, not necessarily post-Columbian contact.

Hickerson believed that an institution like the Midewiwin probably arose out of a time of change and turmoil. He supposed that the post-Columbian fur trade was such a time of change and turmoil. History reflects the contrary, for the days of the early fur trade were a time of prosperity for the Ojibway when they obtained goods that they highly prized in exchange for goods to which they attached little value. They were eager traders who felt they were getting the better of the bargain. However, Ojibway history indicates that they moved west from the St. Lawrence region to escape deadly pestilence in the 14th century. That would have been the Black Death, and most certainly would have been a time of great turmoil. That probably was the time when the Midewiwin was formed. Hickerson's conclusion that the Midewiwin was not Indian in origin is important. It was also true that the Midewiwin was deeply entrenched in the Ojibway culture, and that it consisted of a complex and elaborate ritual. Because it was so complex and extensive, it must have developed from within the tribe; and was not something merely picked up, or adapted from the teachings of short-term missionary activity. To modify old language and create and implant such an institution that then became the leading power center of the tribe, must have taken much time and effort, which would only have been possible from internal sources. In my view, all of those circumstances point to the Midewiwin being developed from within the tribe by Europeans who had become accepted as full and leading members. At one point, to defend his conclusion, Hickerson countered Hoffman's comment about the Midewiwin use of the Cross by asserting that Father Allouez had introduced that symbol to the Ojibway in 1672 (Hickerson 1970: 62). While that may or may not have been the case, it does not prove that the Midewiwin Society was the product of early Catholic missionary efforts. The Midewiwin was a complex system of secret ritual and degrees much like the Masonic Lodge. To contend that such an organization was created by the teachings of Father Allouez based on the possible use of the Cross, is bizarre to say the least. Certainly none of the other Jesuit Fathers introduced secret societies resembling Masonic Lodges into the various Indian tribes that they ministered to.

At first the European Ojibway probably practiced their Midewiwin rituals within their own clan or Totem, however, over time their skill and wisdom earned the respect of whole tribe and so the leaders of the other clans sought and were granted membership in the Midewiwin. That enabled the institution to become the dominant leadership organization for all of the Ojibway. Hickerson's conclusion that the Midewiwin was of European origin is, of course, consistent with my hypothesis, except for the time of the contact. If Hickerson had known of 14th century monks and stone masons from European in close contact with the Indians who became the Ojibway, probably he would have looked to that contact for the source of the Midewiwin.

Eventually the Europeans who had introduced the rituals that became the Midewiwin died, and it was left to their successors to continue that tradition. In my view, it was remarkable that the rituals and religious stories that were passed down remained sufficiently unchanged, so that nineteenth century scholars saw their Biblical nature and twentieth century scholars, like Hickerson and others, concluded that the Midewiwin was of European origin.

Ojibway knowledge
of the Bible

ARREN'S STUDY CLEARLY SHOWS THAT THE OJIB-
way were well versed in the stories found in the Jewish
History or Old Testament of the Bible. Warren wrote:

To satisfy my own curiosity I have sometimes interpreted to
their old men, portions of Bible history, and their expression
is invariably: 'The book must be true, for our ancestors have
told us similar stories, generation after generation, since the
earth was new ...' It is a bold assertion, but it is nevertheless a
true one, that were the traditions of the Ojibway written in
order, and published in a book, it would as a whole bear a
striking resemblance to the Old Testament, and would contain no greater improbabilities than may be accounted for by
the loose manner in which these traditions have been perpetuated; naturally losing force and truth in descending orally
through each succeeding generation. Discard, then, alto-
gether the idea of any connection existing or having existed
between the Ojibway and the Hebrews, and it will be found
difficult to account for all the similarities existing between
many of their rites, customs, and beliefs (Warren 1885: 71).

If we accept Warren's challenge to discard the idea of Hebrew
influence we must look elsewhere for the source. It is my claim
that all of the circumstances, context and geography point to
sources identical to those that produced the KRS.

Peterborough Petroglyphs

THE PETERBOROUGH PETROGLYPHS PROVIDE DRA-
matic and solid evidence of European pre-Columbian
contact in North America, however academic caution
has prevented such a claim from being made because thus far no
one has been able to offer a realistic context for their existence.
The site has about 900 figures carved in a large surface of white
crystalline limestone, sometimes called white marble, located
near Peterborough, Ontario. The site has been dated to a time
after 900 and before 1400 A.D. (Vastokas and Vastokas 1973: 10,
27). The most famous of the Peterborough carvings are those of
ships that resemble Scandinavian ships of the medieval period.

I suggest that the Peterborough site was occupied by the Ojibway soon after their initial migration west from the salt water of
the St. Lawrence. Among these Ojibway were Europeans who
were skilled in the stone carving craft and had European iron
tools to do such carving. They carved the images of Scandinavian
ships found at Peterborough. Some, or all, of those stone carvers
may have been in the party of explorers who had carved the KRS
a few years earlier.

The Peterborough site was not discovered until 1954 because
the whole massive site had been buried and remained so until it
was accidentally found. The burial of the site, probably when the
Ojibway moved on further west, is reminiscent of the burial of
the KRS by the Dakota Indians, probably in both instances to

somehow confine or restrain the potential mystical power that Indians saw in the stone carving. The Peterborough site, comprising about 2500 square feet of limestone surface, was cleared and mapped. A significant aspect of the site is that its location is adjacent to the historic canoe route through Georgian Bay, via the Severn and Trent Rivers, which was the main waterway route used both in prehistoric and fur trade times for east-west travel (Vastokas and Vastokas 1973: 7). That route may well been the route used by the explorers who carved the KRS, and also followed by the Ojibway on their westerly migration from the St. Lawrence. Their western migration suggests that the Ojibway only occupied the Peterborough site for a few years after 1362, but lived there a long enough time to carve those many pictures in stone.

The site was studied by Joan M. Vastokas and Romas K. Vastokas, who published their findings in the book, *Sacred Art of the Algonkians*. If one concluded, as I do, that the pictures of European-style ships found carved in stone at the Peterborough site, were definitely of European origin or influence, then such a finding would instantly change one of the basic assumptions or understandings that most historians have about the European discovery of the New World. However, the Vastokases did not take that major step, and instead concluded, "In this case, however, there is no need to seek explanations of unique and unexpected native cultural forms in terms of outside European influence. What we have here are boat images with deep roots in both North American and Eurasian shamanism" (Vastokas and Vastokas 1973: 126).

My study of the Kensington Rune Stone, however, does permit me to take that step, and claim that the Peterborough Petroglyphs add significant confirmation to my hypothesis that some of the explorers who made the KRS became Ojibway, and played a role in carving the Peterborough Petroglyphs.

The Vastokases' reluctance to claim European origin for the

Boat Petroglyph.
Fourteen boats are among the hundreds of images at the Peterborough, Ontario, Canada, rock art site. This carving, the largest, with an animal headed
prow and a tall mast, measures 3 1/2 feet in length.
Drawing after Vastokas and Vastokas, *Sacred Art of the Algonkians* (1973), p. 122.

boat pictures was surprising considering their enthusiastic description of the boat carvings:

> Of all the images at the Peterborough Petroglyph site, the
> most remarkable and intriguing are a series of fourteen ca-
> noes or boats. Their presence here poses a fascinating icono-
> graphic and historical problem for a number of reasons, the
> most important of which is the fact that they do not seem to
> resemble vessels of native Algonkian or even North Ameri-
> can manufacture (Vastokas and Vastokas 1973: 121).

An unusual "solar disk with radiating beams," as the Vastokases describe it, flying high at the top of the boat's mast, provides a key to confirm the medieval European Church origin of
the carving. Solar disks and sun worship were not a part of Ojibway culture, nor did they use boats for sun worship. The boats are

representations of locally constructed boats of Scandinavian design, only smaller for use on inland waters, such as the Great Lakes. The disk with radiating beams is a representation of a medieval Roman Catholic painting or carving of the Virgin Mary to signify that they sailed under her protection. It was the same figure that the Dakota Indians knew as the White Buffalo Woman. The painting was likely mounted on a long pole which was carried when they marched in a procession, and was tied to the center mast when transported by boat.

The massive number of carvings that comprise the whole Peterborough site, some on top of others, seem to have no central theme or purpose. The Vastokases concluded that pictures as a whole, "do not tell a story" (Vastokas and Vastokas 1973: 46). So, what was the purpose? It is my idea that when the Ojibway settled at the Peterborough site, their group included a few Europeans who had iron tools and who were skilled as stone carvers. As they were not skilled hunters, they could not contribute much in that customary male role, so they became community artists and undertook to teach stone carving to some of the younger boys who were interested, and so the pictures were carved for teaching and amusement. The pictures of the boats, which probably show the type of boat used on their earlier journey to the Lake Superior area, may well have been intended to record evidence of such medium-sized craft and to show that they were used in that area for travel.

The Vastokas study also notes three aspects of the glyphs which I think support my hypothesis. First, they note two styles. In pairs of similar pictures, one is carved with fine and narrow grooves with sharp edges, delicate and life-like, while its counterpart is crudely done in all those respects (Vastokas and Vastokas 1973: 132). A simple explanation for such pairs of pictures would be that the better work was that of the teacher and the simpler was work by the student, who was attempting to copy the work of the teacher. They note that the oldest glyphs are carved in the finer, livelier and more naturalistic style. They were overlapped by the newer crude glyphs (Vastokas and Vastokas 1973: 134). That circumstance shows that the skill of the stone carvers did not improve with practice and time. As the earliest was the best it also means that the more highly skilled stone carver had learned his skill elsewhere and already possessed the ability to do fine work when he arrived. As time passed, the iron tools that the skilled stone carver had brought with him, wore out, and so the later work was done by students with less ability, using crude or worn-out tools, which accounts for the lesser quality of the later work.

The Vastokases were puzzled by the 15 representations of human figures that were included in the mass of carvings, wondering why these relatively simple figures were done as they did nothing, were not obviously linked to other glyphs, and could not be seen to represent spirits. As they were placed apart from other glyphs perhaps these figures were self-portraits of the artists (Vastokas and Vastokas 1973: 78). Probably the answer to the Vastokases' question is, yes. The 15 human figures may well represent the Europeans then surviving. One might ask, if Europeans originated and taught others to do the Petroglyph carvings, why are there no inscriptions or runes? The answer is that only a few medieval Europeans were literate, and stone carvers, who generally were not, only copied inscriptions and runes from a text written by others. Most likely, by the time the Peterborough carvings were made, all of the literate Europeans had died, so the skilled stone carvers who survived were limited to making simple pictures.

However, it may be that the Peterborough carvings do contain a reference to the KRS, which should not be surprising if my hypothesis about who the craftsmen were who carved them is correct. Scholar Barry Fell studied the Peterborough carvings and used them for much of his book, *Bronze Age America*, which relates the carvings to some very ancient Nordic contact. His claims have been rejected by most historians. His study included an attempt to translate many of the carvings, and he interprets some figures to say that a rune stone was carved while the group lingered in a secluded place (Fell 1982: 113). Two of those figures are rectangular in shape and seem to be marked with small dots that could represent the text of an inscription. If one of them was the KRS, perhaps another rune stone is still to be found. While Fell probably was in error in interpreting the Peterborough site as ancient Nordic, he may have been correct in suggesting that the particular figures tell of making rune stones.

The Ojibway
Westward Migration

THE OJIBWAY MIGRATION WEST, FROM THE ST. LAW-
rence, ultimately to Mille Lacs, seems to have a mystical
aspect as if it took place in response to a call to return to the
scene of an ancient drama, long before the Ojibway became aware
of the white man in North America. Such coming of the white men
was prophesied by one of their old men, who warned, ". . . that the
white spirits would come in numbers like sand on the lake shore,
and would sweep the red race from the hunting grounds which the
Great Spirit had given them as an inheritance" (Warren 1885: 117).

They migrated west well ahead of the pressure from post-
Columbian settlement. According to Warren they established
their settlement at La Pointe in Lake Superior in about 1490, two
years before Columbus's first voyage. Their conquest of Lake
Mille Lacs and surrounding territory from the Dakota occurred
in about 1750, a generation before the American Revolution.
Their expansion into Minnesota in the 18th century was at the
expense of the Dakota Indians, who the Ojibway defeated in
many different encounters. Their campaign to take the Mille
Lacs region from the Dakotas was not typical of American Indian warfare, which was usually for revenge and plunder and not
for territory. The Ojibway thought strategically and so seized the
Mille Lacs region, because, as Warren put it, "there is not a spot in
the northwest which an Indian would sooner choose as a home
and dwelling place, than Mille Lacs" (Warren 1885: 156).

→ Part IV ←

The Historical
Consequence

The Open Land

T HE KRS INSCRIPTION REVEALS THAT THE BLACK
Death of 14th century Europe was carried to North
America. It seems evident that the disease spread widely
through the Indian population and was responsible for the sudden
collapse of many of the then more advanced North American Indian cultures. The history of the disease in Europe was that it flared
up frequently for over a century, and presumably it did so also in
North America among the Indian population. The resulting population decline made it appear to Europeans several centuries later,
that they had found a land that was so sparsely occupied, that it was
essentially vacant (Coe, Snow, and Benson 1986: 56, 60, 65). The
absence of a large native population in North America was in contrast to most areas of the world that were colonized; elsewhere
Europeans were able to dominate resident populations, but did not
replace them. Because it was essentially vacant, Europe was at lib-
erty to expand its population into North America.

Archaeologists have found that in many regions of North
America earlier Indian civilizations had once flourished and been
much larger and much more complex, particularly during the first
third of the second millennium. Most significant are the archaeological studies of the Indian Mississippian period, that show that
it began to flourish about 1000 A.D. and went into sharp decline
beginning just before 1400 A.D. One of several large Indian cities
that emerged during that period was located on the Mississippi

River, across from where St. Louis, Missouri now stands. Anthropologists have given it the name of Cahokia. It once had a population estimated to be as high as 25,000 people. Cahokia may have been the destination that the explorers who carved the KRS had intended to reach. A city of that size required an organized system of trade to supply its food and other needs, and a civil structure to keep order and protect itself. Cahokia, and local Indian memory of it, disappeared before post-Columbian settlement began in North America. The reason for the collapse of the Indian civilization of the Mississippian period at Cahokia and at a number of other large Indian centers of population during the Mississippian period, has been one of the unsolved mysteries of anthropology. An epidemic, such as the plague, has always been thought to be a possible explanation for the disappearance, however it was not believed possible that European diseases had crossed the Atlantic. Now that the inscription on the KRS can be understood to describe the presence of the Black Death in North America, it should settle that mystery. Archaeological dating is usually an approximation, however, it seems clear that the collapse of the Indian culture of the Mississippian period came abruptly at about the same time as the date of 1362 on the KRS and also at the same time that the Black Death was devastating Europe.

One Indian historical source that can be interpreted as confirmation of the presence of the Black Death, is the legend of Megis, as recounted by Warren in his *History of the Ojibway*, written in about 1850. Warren quoted the words of an old priest as follows:

'My grandson,' said he, 'the megis [a white sea shell] I spoke of, means the Me-da-we religion. Our forefathers, many string of lives ago, lived on the shores of the Great Salt Water in the east. Here it was, that while congregated in a great town, and while they were suffering the ravages of sickness and death, the Great Spirit, at the intercession of Man-ab-o-sho, the great common uncle of the An-ishin-aub-ag, granted them this rite wherewith life is restored and prolonged. Our forefathers moved from the shores of the great water, and proceeded westward. The Me-da-we lodge was pulled down and it was not again erected, till our forefathers again took a stand on the shores of the great river near where Mo-ne-aung (Montreal) now stands' (Warren 1885: 79).

The legend continues and traces the continued migration of the Ojibway westward, eventually to Fond du Lac (in modern Minnesota) at the western end of Lake Superior (Warren 1885: 79–81). That legendary history points to "suffering the ravages of sickness and death," as the reason for their migration. No doubt the Indians experienced the usual amounts of illness and death, so the sickness and death reported in the legend must have been unusual, more severe, and struck many more victims who would not have been expected to die from illness, just as was the case when the Black Death struck various European communities. It seems clear that their migration legend also relates to the Mundua people and the founding of the Marten Totem as one of the leading totems of the Ojibway, and that the disease that struck the Indians was the same as that which had previously decimated the Mundua. The old priest's reference to the "Great Spirit, at the intercession of Man-ab-o-sho, the great common uncle of the Anish-in-aub-ag," refers to the Christian God and Jesus of the Mundua people. It appears it was the founders of the Me-da-we, or Midewiwin who I believe were the Mundua, that led the newly constituted Ojibway on their migration westward, in the hope that a fresh location would be disease free.

Another confirmation of disease among the Indians in regions proximate to the St. Lawrence in the 14th century that suggests the presence of the Black Death, can be inferred from the story of Hiawatha, as told in the classic *The Iroquois Book of Rites* by Horatio E. Hale, published in 1883. Hale claimed that Hiawatha only took up the diplomatic activity that enshrined his name in legend, after every member of his family and many of his friends and relatives had all been struck dead (Hale 1883: 182, 256). Hiawatha attributed their deaths to the supernatural power or evil eye of Chief Atotarho. Hiawatha's belief that an evil eye caused the disease that struck in the same manner as the European Black Death, was about as sound an explanation for the disease as those advanced by 14th century Europeans. While there has been uncertainty about the time when Hiawatha lived, a number of authorities now place him in the 14th century (Jennings 1993: 77).

American historian Francis Parkman once considered the possibility that the Indians might have repulsed European settlement. He wrote of the Iroquois:

> Could they have read their destiny, and curbed their mad ambition, they might have leagued with themselves four great communities of kindred lineage, to resist the encroachments of civilization, and oppose a barrier of fire to the spread of the young colonies of the east. But their organization and their intelligence were the instruments of a blind frenzy, which impelled them to destroy those whom they might have made their allies in a common cause (Parkman 1867: 703).

In Europe the Black Death's toll negatively impacted all aspects of civil and social structure. In his book, *Plagues and Peoples,* author William H. McNeill makes the point that the English population continued to decline for a century after the first outbreak of the plague, primarily due to continued flare ups. While the early population losses were greatest among the lower classes, the later outbreaks struck a greater number of the educated classes, who could not easily be replaced, thus intensifying the severe economic and social impact of the plague on Northern Europe for many years following the initial onslaught in the 1340's (McNeill 1976: 169).

Presumably the Black Death had at least as severe an impact on the North American Indian world, and it was the Indians' lack of civil structure that rendered them unable to unite against a common danger, If on the other hand the North American Indian population had been significantly larger, such as it would have been if their society, as evidenced in the Mississippian period, had continued to expand and mature from the 14th century onward, it could have developed leadership with the wisdom and ability to unite, as Parkman suggested, and resisted from the start, any attempt by Europeans to occupy North America.

The issues raised in this book should keep anthropologists and historians busy for years in assessing the impact of European medieval contact. One such aspect, which I leave for others to consider, is that the St. Lawrence and Great Lakes waterways presented Europeans with an opportunity to penetrate far into the continent, outflanking Indian tribes on the eastern coast in the post-Columbian period. Possibly the early easy Indian acceptance of that later European entry into the St. Lawrence and Great Lakes regions was due to their earlier involvement with, and adoption of, Europeans in the medieval period.

Lists of Illustrations and Maps

Illustrations:

Maps:

Bibliography

Anderson, Ingvar. 1956. *A History of Sweden*. Weidenfeld and Nicolson, London, England.

Atiya, Aziz S. 1975. "The Crusade in the Fourteenth Century," in *A History of the Crusades*, pp. 3–26. Edited by Harry W. Hazard, University of Wisconsin Press, Madison, WI.

Blegen, Theodore C. 1963. *Minnesota, A History of the State*. University of Minnesota Press, Minneapolis, MN.

Blegen, Theodore C. 1968. *The Kensington Rune Stone. New Light on an Old Riddle*. Minnesota Historical Society Press, St. Paul, MN.

Bray, Edmund C. 1977. *Billions of Years in Minnesota. The Geologic Story of the State*. Science Museum of Minnesota, St. Paul, MN.

Bredero, Adriaan H. 1994. *Christendom and Christianity in the Middle Ages*. Translated by Reinder Bruinsma, William B. Eerdmans Publishing Company, Grand Rapids, MI.

Brower, J. V. and D. I. Bushnell, Jr. 1900. *Mille Lac. Memoirs of Explorations in the Basin of the Mississippi*, Vol. III. H. L. Collins Co., St. Paul, MN.

Brower, J. V. 1901. *Kathio, Memoirs of Explorations in the Basin of the Mississippi*, Vol. IV. H. L. Collins Co., St. Paul, MN.

Brown, Jennifer S. H. and Robert Brightman, editors. 1988. *"The Orders of the Dreamed" George Nelson on Cree and Northern Ojibwa Religion and Myth, 1823*. Minnesota Historical Society Press, St. Paul, MN.

Brown, Joseph Epes. 1982. *The Spiritual Legacy of the American Indian*. Crossroad, New York, NY.

Brown, Joseph Epes. 1953. *The Sacred Pipe. Black Elk's Account of the Seven Rites of the Oglala Sioux.* University of Oklahoma Press, Norman, OK.

Burnet, Sir Macfarlane and David O. White. 1972. *Natural History of Infectious Disease,* 4th Edition. Cambridge University Press, Cambridge, England.

Cantor, Norman F. 1993. *The Civilization of the Middle Ages.* Harper Collins, New York, NY.

Carver, Jonathan. 1784. *Three Years Travels, through the interior parts of North America, for more than five thousand miles.* Joseph Crukshank and Robert Bell, Philadelphia, PA.

Catlin, George. 1841. *Letters and Notes on the Manners, Customs, and Conditions of the North American Indians.* Self published. London, England.

Ceram, C. W. 1971. *The First American. A Story of North American Archaeology.* Harcourt Brace Jovanovich, Inc. New York, NY.

Coe, Michael, Dean Snow and Elizabeth Benson. 1986. *Atlas of Ancient America.* Facts on File, New York, NY.

Crook, Larry D., and Bruce Tempest. 1992. "Plague, A Clinical Review of 27 Cases," June 1992, in *Archives of Internal Medicine,* pp. 1253–1256.

Dorsey, James Owen. 1894. "A Study of Siouxan Cults," *Annual Report of Bureau of American Ethnology XIV,* pp. 361–544. Smithsonian Institution, Washington, DC.

Du Chaillu, Paul. 1882. *The Land of the Midnight Sun.* Harper, New York, NY.

Erdoes, Richard and John (Fire) Lame Deer. 1972. *Lame Deer: Seeker of Visions. The Life of a Sioux Medicine Man.* Simon & Schuster, New York, NY.

Erickson, Carolly. 1976. *The Medieval Vision. Essays in History and Perception.* Oxford University Press, New York, NY.

Fell, Barry. 1982. *Bronze Age America.* Little Brown & Company, Boston, MA.

France, James. 1992. *The Cistercians in Scandinavia.* Cistercian Publications, Inc., Kalamazoo, MI.

Fryxell, Anders. 1844. *History of Sweden.* Richard Bentley, London, England.

Gibbon, Guy E. 1999. "The Pre-History of the Sioux, 9500 B.C.–A.D. 1650," Paper presented at the 57th Annual Plains Anthropological Conference, Sioux Falls, SD.

Gibbon, Guy E. 1974. "A Model of Mississippian Development and its Implications for the Red Wing Area," in *Aspects of Upper Great Lakes Anthropology. Papers in Honor of Lloyd A. Wilford.* Edited by Elden Johnson, pp. 129–137. Minnesota Historical Society, St. Paul, MN.

Gjerset, Knut. 1924. *History of Iceland.* The Macmillan Company, New York, NY.

Gjerset, Knut. 1915. *History of the Norwegian People,* Vol. 2. The Macmillan Company, New York, NY.

Hale, Horatio E. 1883. *The Iroquois Book of Rites.* D. G. Brinton. Philadelphia, PA.

Hall, Robert A. Jr. 1994. *The Kensington Rune-stone, Authentic and Important.* Jupiter Press, Lake Bluff, Ill.

Hall, Robert A. Jr. 1982. *The Kensington Rune-Stone is Genuine.* Hornbeam Press, Inc., Columbia, SC.

Hanson, Barry J. 2001. "The Kensington Runestone. Physical Features, Past and Present," *Journal of the West,* 40:1 (Winter, 2001), 68–80.

Hassrick. Royal B. 1964. *The Sioux: Life and Customs of a Warrior Society.* University of Oklahoma Press, Norman, OK.

Headley, P.C. 1874. *The Island of Fire; or A Thousand Years of the Old Northman's Home.* Lee & Shepard, Boston. MA.

Heer, Friedrich. 1961. *The Medieval World, Europe 1100–1350,* 2 vols. Vienna, Austria.

Helmen, Aksel, N.D. *Hadeland, Litt om Søsterkirkene, Granavoldens historie og andre historiske steder på Hadeland.* A. S. Hadeland's Trykkeri. Brandbu, Norway.

Hennepin, Louis. 1699. *A New Discovery of a Vast Country in America, extending above Four Thousand Miles, Between New France and New Mexico.* Printed by Henry Bonwicke, at the Red Lion in St. Paul's Church-Yard. London, England.

Hickerson, Harold. 1970. *The Chippewa and Their Neighbors: A Study in Ethnohistory.* Holt, Rinehart and Winston, Inc., New York, NY.

Hill, Ruth Beebe. 1979. *Hanta Yo.* Doubleday & Co., Inc., Garden City, NJ.

Hirst, L. Fabian. 1953. *The Conquest of Plague.* Clarendon Press, Oxford, England.

Hoffman, W. J. 1891. "The Mide-wiwin or 'Grand Medicine Society' of the Ojibway," *Annual Report of the Bureau of American Ethnology, VII* (1885–1886), pp. 143–300. Smithsonian Institution, Washington, DC.

Holand, Hjalmar. 1932. *The Kensington Stone: A Study in Pre-Columbian American History.* Privately printed. Ephraim, WI.

Holler, Clyde. 1995. *Black Elk's Religion.* Syracuse University Press, Syracuse, NY.

Howard, James H. 1979. *The British Museum Winter Count.* Occasional Paper No. 4. British Museum, London, England.

Ingstad, Helge. 1966. *Land under the Pole Star.* St. Martin's Press, New York, NY.

Ingstad, Helge. 1969. *Westward to Vinland.* St. Martin's Press, New York, NY.

Innis, Harold A. 1940. *The Cod Fisheries.* Yale University Press, New Haven, CT.

Jennings, Francis. 1993. *The Founders of America.* Norton, New York, NY.

Kalm, Peter. 1937. *The America of 1750. Peter Kalm's Travels in North America.* Edited by Adolph B. Benson. Wilson-Erickson, Inc. New York, NY.

Keating, William H. 1825. *Narrative of an Expedition to the Sources of St. Peter's River, Lake Winnepeek, Lake of the Woods,* etc. 2 vols. G. B. Whittaker, London, England.

Landes, Ruth. 1968. *The Mystic Lake Sioux: Sociology of the Mdewakantonwan Santee.* University of Wisconsin Press, Madison WI.

Landes, Ruth. 1970. *The Prairie Potawatomi. Tradition and Ritual in the Twentieth Century.* University of Wisconsin Press, Madison, WI.

Larson, Constant., editor. 1916. *History of Douglas and Grant Counties, Minnesota: Their People, Industries and Institutions.* B. F Bowen & Co., Indianapolis, IN.

Laurin, Carl G. 1922. "A Survey of Swedish Art," in *Scandinavian Art* by Carl Laurin, Emil Hannover & Jens Thiis, pp. 37–237. Oxford University Press, New York, NY.

Lefrock, Jack L., Abdolghadler Molavi and Arnold Lentneck. 1984, "Yersinia Pestis," in Levison, Matthew E., editor. *The Pneumonias, Clinical Approaches to Infectious Diseases of the Lower Respiratory Tract,* pp. 340–342. Boston, MA.

Lekai, Louis J. 1953. *The White Monks. A History of the Cistercian Order.* Cistercian Fathers, Okauchee, WI.

Luddy, Rev. Ailbe J. 1932. *The Order of Citeaux.* M. H. Gill and Son, Ltd., Dublin, Ireland.

McNeill, William H. 1976. *Plagues and Peoples.* Anchor Press, New York, NY.

Mackey, Albert. 1898. *The History of Freemasonry.* The Masonic History Company, New York, NY.

Macy, Dennis W., D.V.M. 1989. "Plague," *Current Veterinary Therapy,* pp. 1088–1089, William B. Saunders, Philadelphia, PA.

Mallery, Garrick. 1893. "Picture Writing of the American Indians," *Annual Report of the Bureau of American Ethnology, X,* (1888–1889) pp. 266–328, Smithsonian Institution, Washington, DC.

Mallery, Garrick. 1886. "Pictographs of the North American Indians: A Preliminary Paper," *Annual Report of the Bureau of American Ethnology, IV* (1882–1883), pp. 1–256, Smithsonian Institution, Washington, DC.

Mason, Ronald J. 1981. *Great Lakes Archaeology.* Academic Press, New York, NY.

Mather, David. "The Headless Bison Calf from the Fingerson Mound, Pope County, Minnesota," Paper presented at Joint Midwest Archaeological/Plains Anthropological Conference. St. Paul, Minnesota, Nov. 9–12, 2000.

McKenney, Thomas and James Hall. *History of the Indian Tribes of North America. 1836–1844.* Key and Biddle. Philadelphia, PA.

Melberg, Hakon. 1949. *Origin of the Scandinavian Nations and Languages,* 2 vols. Halden, Norway.

Morison, Samuel Eliot. 1971. *The European Discovery of America, the Northern Voyages. A.D. 500–1600.* Oxford University Press, New York, NY.

Morse, Eric W. 1969. *Fur Trade Canoe Routes of Canada/Then and Now.* Queen's Printer and Controller of Stationery, Ottawa, Ontario, Canada.

Mowat, Farley. 1965. *Westviking. The Ancient Norse in Greenland and North America.* Little Brown & Company, Boston, MA.

Neihardt, John. 1932. *Black Elk Speaks, Being the Life Story of a Holy Man of the Oglala Sioux.* William Morrow, New York, NY.

Neill, Rev. Edward Duffield. 1882. *The History of Minnesota from the Earliest French Explorations to the Present Time,* 4th Ed. Minnesota Historical Company, Minneapolis, MN.

Nielsen, Richard. 1987. "The Aberrant Letters on the Kensington Runestone ," Vol. 16, *Occasional Papers of the Epigraphic Society,* San Diego, CA.

Nielsen, Richard. 1988. "Appendix II to Linguistic Evidence Which Supports that the Kensington Runestone is Genuine," Vol. 17, *Occasional Papers of the Epigraphic Society,* San Diego, CA.

Nielsen, Richard. 1986. "The Arabic Numbering System on the Kensington Runestone," Vol. 15, *Occasional Papers of the Epigraphic Society,* San Diego, CA.

Nielsen, Richard. 1989. "Linguistic Evidence Which Supports That the Kensington Runestone is Genuine," Vol. 18, *Occasional Papers of the Epigraphic Society,* San Diego, CA.

Nielsen, Richard. 2000. "Early Scandinavian Incursions into the Western States," *Journal of the West,* 39: 1 (January 2000).

Ojakangas, Richard W., and Charles L. Matsch. 1982. *Minnesota's Geology.* University of Minnesota Press, Minneapolis, MN.

Paper, Jordan. 1988. *Offering Smoke. The Sacred Pipe and Native American Religion.* University of Idaho Press, Moscow, ID.

Parker, John. 1976. *The Journals of Jonathan Carver and Related Documents, 1766–1770.* Minnesota Historical Society Press, St. Paul, MN.

Parkman, Francis. 1867. *The Jesuits in North America in the Seventeenth Century.* Little, Brown & Co., Boston, MA.

Pennington, M. Basil. 1991. *Light From the Cloister.* Paulist Press, Mahwah, NJ.

Radisson, Pierre Esprit. 1961. *The Exploration of Pierre Esprit Radisson.* Edited by Arthur T. Adams. Ross & Haines, Minneapolis, MN.

Reman, Edward. 1990. *The Norse Discoveries and Explorations in America.* Dorset Press, New York, NY.

Riegert, Wilbur A. 1975. *Quest for the Pipe of the Sioux: as Viewed from Wounded Knee.* J. M. Fritze, Rapid City, SD.

Riggs, Stephen. 1890. *Mary and I. Forty Years with the Sioux.* W. G. Holmes, Chicago, IL.

Riggs, Stephen, editor. 1852. *Grammar and Dictionary of the Dakota Language.* Contributions to Knowledge, Vol. 4. Smithsonian Institution, Washington, DC.

Riggs, Stephen, 1893. *Dakota Grammar, Texts and Ethnography.* U.S. Geographical and Geological Survey of the Rocky Mountain Region, Contributions to North American Ethnology, Vol. 9. Washington, DC.

Robinson, Doane. 1904. *A History of the Dakota or Sioux Indians: From their Earliest Traditions and First Contact with White Men to the Final Settlement of the Last of Them upon Reservations and the Consequent Abandonment of the Old Tribal life.* South Dakota Historical Collections, Vol. 2, Part II.

Schmalz, Peter. 1991. *The Ojibwa of Southern Ontario.* The University of Toronto Press, Toronto, Ontario, Canada.

Schwartz, George M. 1949. *The Geology of the Duluth Metropolitan Area.* University of Minnesota Press, Minneapolis, MN.

Schwartz, George M. and George A. Thiel. 1963. *Minnesota's Rocks and Waters: A Geological Story.* University of Minnesota Press, Minneapolis, MN.

Scott, Franklin D. 1977. *Sweden: The Nation's History.* University of Minnesota Press, Minneapolis, MN.

Sims, Paul Kibler, and G. B. Morey, eds. 1972. *Geology of Minnesota, a Centennial Volume in Honor of George M. Schwartz.* Minnesota Geological Survey, St. Paul, MN.

Spencer, Arthur. 1974. *Gotland.* David & Charles, Vancouver, B.C. Canada.

Steltenkamp, Michael F. 1993. *Black Elk: Holy Man of the Oglala.* University of Oklahoma Press, Norman, OK.

Steltenkamp, Michael F. 1982. *The Sacred Vision: Native American Religion and its Practice Today.* Paulist Press, Ramsey, NJ.

Thomas, Sidney J. 1941. "A Sioux Medicine Bundle," *American Anthropologist,* n.s. 43, pp. 605–609.

Thompson, Gunnar. 1996. *The Friar's Map of Ancient America—1360 AD. The Story of Nicholas of Lynn and the Franciscan Map of America.* Laura Lee Productions, Bellevue, WA.

Twigg, Graham. 1984. *The Black Death, A Biological Reappraisal.* Schocken Books, New York, NY.

Vastokas, Joan M. and Romas K. Vastokas. 1973. *Sacred Art of the Algonkians, a Study of the Peterborough Petroglyphs*. Mansard Press, Peterborough, Ontario, Canada.

Wahlgren, Erik. 1958. *The Kensington Stone: A Mystery Solved.* University of Wisconsin Press, Madison, WI.

Walker, James R. 1980. *Lakota Belief and Ritual*. Edited by Raymond J. DeMallie and Elaine A. Jahner. University of Nebraska Press, Lincoln, NE.

Walker, James R. 1982. *Lakota Society*. Edited by Raymond J. DeMallie. University of Nebraska Press. Lincoln, NE.

Walker, James R. 1983. *Lakota Myth*. Edited by Elaine A. Jahner. University of Nebraska Press, Lincoln, NE.

Wallace, Douglas C. 1998. "Global Mitochondrial DNA Variation and the Origin of Native Americans." Electronically published by the Center for Molecular Medicine, Emory University, Atlanta, GA.

Warren, William W. 1885. "History of the Ojibway People." *Minnesota Historical Society Collections*, Vol. 5. St. Paul, MN.

West, Geoffrey, editor. 1992. *Black's Veterinary Dictionary*. 17th Ed., Barnes & Noble, New York, NY.

Wilford, Lloyd A., Elden Johnson and Joan Vicinus. 1969. *Burial Mounds of Central Minnesota; Excavation Reports*. Minnesota Historical Society, St. Paul, MN.

Willard, Jon. 1964. *Lac Qui Parle and the Dakota Mission*. Lac Qui Parle Historical Society, Madison, MN.

Winchell, N. H. 1911. *The Aborigines of Minnesota. A Report Based on the Collections of Jacob V. Brower and on the Field Surveys and Notes of Alfred J. Hill and Theodore H. Lewis.* Minnesota Historical Society, St. Paul, MN.

Winchell, N. H. 1915. "The Kensington Rune Stone; Preliminary Report to the Minnesota Historical Society by the Museum Committee," *Minnesota Historical Society Collections*, Vol. XV, pp. 221–286. St. Paul, MN.

Wise, Jennings C. 1931. *The Red Man in the New World Drama: A Politico-Legal Study with a Pageantry of American Indian History*. W. F. Roberts Company, Washington, DC.

Wright, H. E. 1990. *Geologic History of Minnesota Rivers*. Minnesota Geological Survey Educational Series 7, St. Paul, MN.

Wub-e-ke-niew. 1995. *We Have the Right to Exist.* Black Thistle Press, New York, NY.

Zalar, Michael A. 2001. "16th Century Cartography Plat Maps, and the Kensington Runestone," *Journal of the West*, 40: 1 (Winter 2001) 62–67.

Ziegler, Philip. 1971. *The Black Death.* Harper & Row, Torchbooks, New York, NY.

_____. U.S. Navy Hydrographic Office. 1917. *St. Lawrence Pilot, the Gulf and River St. Lawrence.* 4th Edition., H.O.100, Government Printing Office, Washington, DC.

Index